My Dog Eats Plant Pots

HANNAH TAYLOR

Dear Whoever

If you have had a cursory glance at what lies within, and might be thinking how can she be so rude about real people, please let me say that I am fully aware of the law of this fine land. It is not my intention to defame, insult or cause harm to anyone. I have written this book using contemporaneous notes, emails and my memories. I believe what I have written to be fact, which I can back up with reams of paperwork. This is my truth and my honest (very honest) opinion. If I could put myself in my son's head and tell you his story I would, but I would never try. I can only tell you about my experiences from my perspective. I have tried hard to anonymise everything, sometimes that might seem harsh, and distanced, but if you think you recognise yourself, I hope you are one of the good guys. If not, sorry about whatever moniker I have given you. The intention was genuinely to ensure you remained incognito. You don't want to be within these pages? I don't want to be either.

H

I Am Normal ... Honest

If you could choose a book... any book ... which, if some bugger hadn't written first, you would have like to have penned, what would it be? I mean there was a point in my life when it would have been Bridget Jones Strikes Back, or Shopaholic goes to the Selfridges Shoe Sale, or maybe even something slightly more academic (maybe about the anthropomorphic tendencies of those humans blessed to have a Dennis Healy eyebrowed, ever so slightly disapproving of your drinking habits stinky old hound in their lives)... or something based on one of your most scintillating skills or hobbies ... Box Tree Topiary for Beginners, or Wine Glass Bottoms I Have Observed. I'm only asking because they say everyone has got a book in them don't they? And I was just thinking that if I had all the time in the world, and could sit in my writing chalet by the sea, with my ancient typewriter, the coastal breeze blowing my voile curtains just enough, the only sounds being the odd squawk from a hungry seagull, the waves crashing towards the beach, and the ozone fresh scent surrounding me, I might be able to lose myself enough to write that magnum opus. How wonderful that would be, and how fulfilling.

The problem is I don't live anywhere near the ocean, the only birds I have seen today are two randy pigeons on the phone wire, and the predominant sound if I do actually open a window and let my curtains flap, is the traffic speeding past my door, with the wafting aroma of car exhaust fumes. I also like to pretend that I am very busy, and my brain is too full to fit any other pastime in. If I am tapping away at my computer though (not typewriter sadly), at least I look like I am doing some very important work-related exercise, when actually I am sat here talking to you. Dreaming about what book you would want to write, is sadly just that, a dream, and probably in no way related to the one that actually comes out when you start doing it. May I say with that in mind, that this is not the book I think I want to write, I don't even know quite why I am doing it. But now I have started thinking about it I can't stop. I kind of want to tell our tale, which is by the way not a grand work of fiction but my truth. It's not a question of better out than in, because it will still have happened. The thing is when I was looking for someone who might have had the same experience as us, I found reading other peoples' sorry accounts of similar events to be rather helpful, partly because it meant I knew I wasn't finally going completely mad. My 78 year old Dad saw this pile of paper and asked me if I had really written a book. I said "erm… yes… but it's not much fun. And I swear a bit." And he read it anyway. And said "you should get that out there, someone might be interested". So if you are that someone then here you go.

It has been a shite few years, and if I could turn back the clock and do things differently I definitely would, one way or another. I say this having spent at least 24 hours in the last week chuckling about my ever so, and sometimes scarily observant and nosy tweenie who, having overheard an old friend, not seen for two years commenting on how his wife had lost her marbles, piped up "I've got marbles, will she want some of mine?" and some time later appeared at the door with a presentation box tied in a bow, labelled "Marbles", containing a choice selection of your finest glass spherical playthings. My lovely old friend spent the next two hours trying to work out how to explain this gift to his wife when he got home, without dropping himself in it.

I am an adopter. I have two adopted children. One is she, of marble fame. The other is my son. Who doesn't live with us any more. I'm trying desperately not to blame anyone for that. Including myself. There's no point in that is there? I'm also not trying to justify anything, for some kind of therapeutic end. I could never do that. I could have been a different person and then things might not have gone the way they did, but sorry to say I am me. I'm a different version of me than I was before this all happened. Probably not a better version. I know I've got more grey hair, more wrinkles, and a bigger bum. Those things are obvious. What you can't see is the mess inside my head. And that is probably a good thing.

Right, must get on with it. Here is my disclaimer. I am afraid I know I am about to criticise some very important people, who are commonly known as Social Workers. If you are one, do stop reading now, because I really don't want to offend you. Sorry about the names I gave you to distinguish one from another. I do get that there are some very wonderful ones out there. I believe I even contemplated that line of work myself once. Thank feck I didn't do anything about it. I wouldn't like myself very much now. Or anyone else for that matter. But I cannot imagine a more demoralising job than one where you see the lows of peoples' lives on a daily basis. What does that tell you about existence? What's the point? Surely they can't all go home at night and revel in how wonderful their own lives are, because they have just spent the day engulfed in other people's misery and misfortune? Does their supervision help? I do hope so for their sakes. Who knows. What I do know is that I have met so many now that I have forgotten most of their names. Some darlings are etched so hard into my brain that I can never forget, not necessarily the details of them but the feelings that their very presence or even the thought of it, came to evoke in me. In our dealings they have all been most keen to be invited into our house, drink our loose leaf lapsang souchong, or our latest finest columbian, eat our custard creams, and sit for hours whilst we conversed, so delightfully polite. They have then gone away, back to Social Service Headquarters to write things up, in their own way, with their own spin, and sometimes in spite of anything that has been discussed chez nous. Sometimes this is OK, a lot of times this unbeknown to us seems to have been at our expense. I sound paranoid, I sound bitter. I am I suppose. Social Workers. Social. Workers. I used to see them as a means to an end, as a positive factor in our lives. Now if I hear the term I come out in a cold sweat, or develop momentary Tourettes. Speaking of which, I think I mentioned I do occasionally lapse into a vernacular, which also may offend. Scuse my French, I can't help it. Sorry Mother.

Can I just say right now, I'm not expecting you to like me. I can't make you. Sometimes I don't like myself. I kind of do, and then I don't again. I sometimes think I'm a shit. And then again I'm OK, I'm not that bad, I'll do. It does help doesn't it that if you're being told something by someone, that if you like them you want to listen? And in a story where the person regaling the tale is someone you can relate to, or is funny, entertaining, engaging, or fascinating, then you tend to want to hear more. Well, sorry to disappoint. I am a bit Nelly normal. I wish I had a superpower, or a scintillating background, but I am just a normal girl from a normal place, in a normal town. Sometimes I eat straight from the fridge when no-one's looking. I believe Elvis was the King of Rock and Roll. I like wine and chocolate. I like cars. I happily binge watch the original Star Trek. I learned to play a funny little musical instrument late in life and can't understand why I have never been snapped up as the next big thing. Actually I know why. I make up for my lack of talent with playing comically, or just at top volume, which is not widely appreciated. I have a Youtube channel, and I have two subscribers! OK one is actually me, but someone stalks me. I appreciate dental floss. I like growing potatoes. I have a thing about ornaments and trinkets, but my dusting of them leaves a lot to be desired. I ought to undertake therapy to curb my shoe habit. I should speak my degree-level French better, but my pub-learned German is superb. I love a fancy-dress party, my favourite was a Dick Whittington affair, although I lost my hat on the way home, and found it two weeks later in a hedge miles off my route. A fact that still puzzles me.

I used to be a librarian, and am very good at shushing, although arguably it was me making most of the racket. Then I accidently became a hospital support worker, so I too have seen people at their best and worst. I would like to upsticks and move somewhere remote where I would own my own little tractor, and we would live on my garden produce, homemade bread, jam and wine, and collect eggs from my interesting collection of chickens, but we are too normal for that. Sometimes I forget to buy dog food, and my dog eats cheese sandwiches. My little plantpot eating dog who is currently defying medical science by just existing. She has a tumour bless her. And had two weeks to live, over a year ago. I do wonder if this is due to the homeopathic use of turmeric in her food. Either this is some kind of miracle, although dealing with the doings of a dog with a yellow spice habit is not always pleasant, or she is just a stubborn old bag. Or both. The same would be, and probably has been, said about me. The stubborn old bag bit, not the spice habit.

I feel like I ought to make some apologies in advance for this story. I'm not frigging apologising to any aforementioned social worker. They do a job, just like I or you do a job. They get paid. If they don't like it, then don't do it. Actually, I might say sorry to some of them. The ones who I haven't met. If you have ignored my advice and are still reading this, I really don't mean to be offensive, I haven't met you. It's not personal, and this story isn't about you. It's about me, and my shit, not you and yours. I like fairy tales, don't we all? I always say to my daughter when she bursts into tears as the evil baddies mistreat the favourite cat belonging to the beautiful princess, "you know it will all turn out right in the end darling". "Always look on the bright side", "it could be worse, you could get run over by a bus tomorrow". Oh yes, I'm full of it. Unfortunately this is no fairy tale, so also apologies in advance for the utterly demoralising beginning and middle, I'll come on to the end. I don't mean to be morbid, but I think some truth needs telling. It's good for your karma, well mine anyway, and I will get it off my chest, be ranty, let it out, release the demons. Then if anyone, like me, is having a funny five minutes and looking to see if someone has had the same experience, they might find my ramblings, and then I will have done a good thing and they can be the second member of my "Haven't Actually Gone Completely Mad Society". In the middle of putting all of this down on paper … well the screen equivalent of paper, I decided it was important to really try to see if anyone else had been so blatantly honest about their similar experiences. To my knowledge, not really, that is to say not in the same way. I read a book or two thinking at the very least I might be able to find some juicy quotes, but unfortunately I ended up cross. Because it was different. And the last one I think I threw away in a huff, after I took a dislike to the author, and what they were telling me about their actions, reasons or justifications. Maybe if I didn't know me I would do the same with this. But then again having put it all in words now I can see that we all have a truth, and it's what makes us us. And this is my truth, my words, my story.

What is a good story? What did they say at school? A beginning, a middle and an end. Say what you are going to say, say it, say what you have said, and don't use clichés. I can't do that, sorry (note to self to stop apologising). I have realised I must overuse clichés in my daily speech, maybe there's a self-help group for that. And the story has not ended. I have got a beginning, and a sort of middle … but no end in sight yet. No light at the end of the tunnel. But the tunnel is the most interesting and challenging one I've been through. I must also say this isn't my husband's story. Don't get me wrong, he was there, at the beginning, and in the middle, and he is still here now. And he experienced everything I am about to tell you too. But he experienced it in his own way, and takes from it his own thing. We are a couple, a pair, a duo, a double act. Eric and Ernie (I'm Eric). Fred and Ginger (I'm almost Ginger, but don't hold it against me). Apple crumble and custard (definitely the custard). But it doesn't mean we think the same, or act the same. That's the beauty of it isn't it? Bouncing off each other, complimentary characteristics, or even opposites attract. So for whatever reason it works. Mostly. But I can't speak for him, and normally if I try I get it horribly wrong, even though we have been married long enough to forget anniversaries, to be complacent sometimes. I would not dream of trying to explain to you how events have impacted on him. He needs to tell you that himself. But he probably won't. So, may I take you on my journey? Well you're with me now aren't you, so shall we begin?

Go On Then, Prove Yourselves...

Right how do I start this thing. I'm thinking, never mind the scene setting, let's get straight to the point. In a shellnut, as our Italian friend used to say, we, that's Hub and me, and Dog (I'm not going to speak for her either, love that hairy little curry scented nutter), adopted two little children seven years ago, and heartachingly emotionally battered and bruised three years ago we gave our son over and entrusted his care going forwards to Social Services to do what they promised with the rest of his life. There I go, sounding bitter again. That's because I am, I know I am, and I can't shake that feeling, I don't know if I ever will, and that makes it worse. I don't know where the story ends, I don't know if I will ever be satisfied with my own actions, the response from people around me, enough at least to feel that somehow a positive has come out of this for him.

This "thing" that happened, that nobody wants to talk about. Nobody is really sure of the percentage of people that this thing happens to. That's because they don't publish figures on it. People have tried to do studies about it, to get it out there, known about, work out why it happens. Have a look. You will find the figures are old, startling, but old. The Beeb did a bit on the topic in 2017, and reckoned that somewhere between 3.2% and 9% of adoptions fail. Some article I read the other day suggested higher. So there are no published statistics on adoption breakdown. Bugger, I'm not supposed to use that phrase, it's officially called "disruption". Does that figure sound a lot to you? Too bloody right it does. And it is a lot. An effing lot. Not that it will, or indeed should stop anyone considering adoption, there will always be children who need a family and always families who need them. I read something the other day about how adoption has changed, and that once many adoptions happened because of the taboo of being an unmarried mother, and now many result from the neglect of children and removal of them from birth families by Social Services, at whatever point they identify a child cannot live there any more. This piece was suggesting that this has changed massively the needs of those children, and this is an unpredicted societal change, that has been too slowly recognised. If it goes wrong I know for sure that the people, who may well have worn rose tinted spectacles, who may have thought they have superhuman emotional strength, or for whom a child was supposed to complete their lives, should never blame themselves for the fallout from damage done by the past, by other peoples' mistakes, cruelty or simple lack of help. I say that, but then I go around thinking, I was meant to make it better and I didn't.

I was naïve, blinded by hope and in love with the idea of being a parent, a mum, with the thought of happy Enid Blytonesque adventuring going on right before my very eyes, me thinking I know all about this, I've read it all. Let's have lashings and lashings of ginger beer to celebrate this idyllic existence, where I will be some super cool child-centred, uber funky dude with kids who are polite, bright and above all happy. Don't roll your eyes, I read all the stuff, I can recite you the acronyms, I can tell you all about what the impact of early trauma can be… I can also now tell you about secondary trauma too if you like. But seriously do you think that given a chance you wouldn't think you could sort it, you could be therapeutic enough to ride the storms, get over the hurdles, beat the demons?

The context of our story is not unusual. We were living the life of Reilly (whoever he was, I'm jealous). Husband was in the Services, I had some quite demanding but hugely satisfying jobs where I could get them, being what they used to call a "wife of". Living abroad we wives were known as "Dependants". Yes really, in this day and age! We had friends, fun, parties, holidays, the bonkers Dog, no worries. Oh, except the unmentionable one. We didn't seem to be able to have children. We did want them, and being those Double Income No Kids Yet types, we normally just went and got whatever it was we wanted. That's what you do, when you don't have to think about anyone else. But not being able to do a simple thing like make a child became an overwhelmingly consuming problem. IVF? Tried that. Didn't work. I don't know why, neither does anyone else. So what were we going to do about it?

Well, we weren't strangers to adoption and its ups and downs. It was in our family, lots of it, adopted brothers, sisters, nieces. Oh, didn't we think we knew it all. Still it meant it wasn't a taboo subject, and I guess made it seem rather ordinary as we were surrounded by it. So we went for it, "we'll do that then", sort of thing. "But, you can't just do it", they said. You have to "grieve" for the child you never had for a year first, oh, and settle down, put down some roots. Seriously? Load of guff. These were the Services advisors on adoption. How the heck did they think we were going to be settled when the demands of the job meant you move all the sodding time? First experience of social workers did not go well. Put me in a right old huff I can tell you. But those well-intentioned lovelies were a means to an end, so off we popped to get over our virtual loss of the non-existent child, and did some more living the DINKY life, rode motorbikes, went trekking, drank lots of cocktails, worked hard, played hard, Reilly might even have been jealous of me. What was it my husband used to say..? "If you're not living life on the edge, you're taking up too much space"!

We also moved back to England. I flipping hated it. We lived in a non-descript Services Quarter, in a part of town we couldn't afford to live in any other way, but the sense of community that we had felt abroad, had gone. It was all about work, work and then some more work, and people seemed so insular. We carried on there for a year or so, getting more and more obsessed about house hunting, although not taking it very seriously. But then bugger me we saw her, a beautiful slightly bedraggled 1930s affair, like a flapper the morning after the night before (I relate to that). I did say flapper..! The Estate Agent didn't want us to see her, I suppose he thought we might think he was a bit doolally. But we walked inside and immediately knew she could be turned back into a grande dame, she still vaguely had her looks, they just needed tidying up (a lot). So we bought it. Dog loved it, she spent hours gazing out of the low windows, front paws upon the window sill. At the end of the day, as long as there are cats trespassing into your garden, and you've got your big beanbag and your humans, anywhere can be home. But this one had special doggy-height windows onto the big world.

During the renovation proceedings (which by the way are still not over, hey, we've only been here ten years, these things take time and life's a work in progress), we made it child friendly, as you do, no sharp corners allowed, window locks obligatory, knife drawer security installed, carpets advantageous, working toilet kind of helpful, that sort of thing. Husband bought £85 a roll wallpaper, and how glorious it was, patterned like the Sydney Opera House on speed, bronzed, silvered, very art deco. It was like buying a couture dress for the old lady. I painted over it in the end. Too bloody dark. We did all the right things, not necessarily in the right order. And we finally got on the rollercoaster of the adoption process, with its good bits and scary bits. We went to a meeting and behaved ourselves. They said we could apply. They took us seriously, maybe because we are very good at filling in forms. Rather dauntingly we met our first sensible social worker. She was weirdly posh. And quite floaty, but massively practical. She was the one who first used the phrase “poor man’s nanny” to describe the use of the telly to control children. We liked her. She got us going, gave us hope that one day, just maybe...

We were allowed to go on a course after a while. That was kind wasn’t it? I like courses. Especially ones with nice buffets. It must have cost a blooming fortune. That might be where my arse expansion began. We all ate lots. With about six other couples we were encouraged to talk about childlessness, adoption, trauma, education, abuse, share our thoughts. Gosh it was such fun. I am fibbing here. I hated it, you feel like you are being observed, and it was our first experience of having to make things a bit too public for my liking. The nice buffet lunches did not make up for it. Looking back you’re told all sorts of generic things that might happen, and discuss possible consequences with, in our case, a bunch of educated individuals, some of whom had children already, some didn’t, nothing more in common than that wish to give a home to a child who needed it. Let’s not pretend though. Those who had children didn’t sit down and say “we’ve done such a good job with these, we must find a child who hasn’t been so lucky and give them a family that works”, and we didn’t say “we’ve got so much we must share it with someone less fortunate than ourselves". We were all desperate in our own ways, and they, sorry I mean Social Services (I think we are supposed to call them Childrens Services these days, but I will refer to them as The SS from now on, because it makes at least one corner of my mouth turn up) played on that.

I don't know how many people turn round at that stage and back out, we were wrung out after the two days, no statistics on that, don't know how many people really take it in and understand. I guess many of us say we do, because it was just a hurdle we needed to leap over in the adoption steeplechase. I suppose it was our first real introduction to people telling us the good, the bad and the ugly. And I am being slightly facetious, we did think hard, and work hard to understand these new concepts of dreadfulness that we were being told about, which didn't fit with our own life experiences, so had never really been a reality before. Like foetal alcohol syndrome and attachment disorders. Even with the adoption experience of our immediate family. Of course it didn't put us off. We had confidence on our side.

So, big tick, passed that one. No-one kicked us out, called us impostors, told us we didn't seem right. I should think so too. Out of our comfort zone we had performed admirably I thought. When I think about it, I suppose everyone else was in the same boat. No matter what your background, what experience you have, placed in those kind of situations you must all feel rather uncomfortable, because in reality you haven't yet been approved as actual adopters, no-one has actually said you could do it, and put you forward.

Anyway, having proved our prowess on enough occasions, we were allocated another member of The SS. She was very nice, very earnest, very malleable, couldn't spell, and she definitely liked our custard creams a lot. A good job she did, seeing as we had to meet her on a weekly basis at home to go through the reams and reams of paperwork and rather probing questions about all aspects of what made us "us". She would arrive on our drive, and fall out of her little Nissan Micra, she was a bit too big for it really, so I would watch it happen every time she arrived, it helped to relax me on her visits. We had managed to persuade her that because we were both working, we couldn't take the entire afternoon off for this once a week, so she came in the early evening mostly. I was working in a school at this point, and time off was so precious. Basically not allowed, unless you were half dead. So I had had to tell the Bursar, and via her, the Head, what we were up to. That is public. That sort of gives people a licence to ask about it, and quite frankly I didn't want to talk about it. But still, it meant that when I needed to leave a bit early to fit in with The SS timetable I could do it. And do it I did. So did husband. To be fair his job was slightly more high pressured than mine, in a different way anyway, so leaving early was a big thing. But every week we were at home, waiting to receive. The little Nissan Micra would come to a jerky halt on the drive, I would have been pacing the house for half an hour at this point. I would watch her fall out of it, with all her bags and bits of paper. And she would plod up the drive. Tea and biscuits aplenty, she would start her interrogation. She was like the Johnny English of the Spanish Inquisition (Juan Espanol?).

There comes a point when you have told a stranger so much about your personal goings on that you feel like there's a third person in your marriage, you know, you tell your other half things you wouldn't dream of telling anyone else, and ever so slightly under and over-exaggerate, well she was like that., she somehow got it out of us. But very nice as I said, lovely girl. That painful process took a long time, I can't even remember how long, but months and months. I needed lots of time off. They must have been so pissed off with me at work. It was actually quite a good job I had managed to get by then, and I was pretending to be committed, but probably would have been better actually being committed as I was so stressed out by all the intrusiveness of the process we were going through. I started to feel like they must have thought that I had taken the job on false pretences, if my intention was to do this all along, but they were so supportive of me, I was somewhat humbled by it. At the same time, we couldn't keep making excuses to friends and family. My mother in law, bless her, and love her to bits, she is genuinely brilliant, but one for speaking her mind, had from the very early days of our relationship wondered out loud when we were going to produce her a grandchild. The adoption in the family I spoke about? That was her. My husband was the only child she had given birth to. The others were adopted from the 1960s to the 1980s. She and my father in law (love him too, he is quietly amazing), were of the generation where you believed you should do good by others, they were a bit left wing, and I don't know if that played a part but I think the whole thing caused within their family all manner of upset, some of it unforgiveable, and irreversible. We did feel that she would understand our situation, and we decided we needed to go properly public, and told them.

Of course once it starts impacting on other people, then it needs to be talked about, and can you imagine saying then "I've decided not to do it as it's too difficult", or "I can't be bothered to answer all those horrible questions any more, they're just so rude"? I don't think so. So despite the probing and the constant questioning of our lives, on we cracked.

Ve Vill Now Probe You

You then start with The SS going into the realms of family and friends and your “support network”. How are they going to react if it all happens? Have you told them? Not being funny but who effing cares? You don’t ask around before you get pregnant to see if anyone doesn’t think it’s a good idea. “Oh, you don’t think we’re ready? Oh well in that case we’ll not do it.” But we had pre-empted it somewhat by already telling them in our own way. Dog was very supportive, always the element of normality in proceedings, carried on pooing in inappropriate places, chewing on my plant pots, sleeping on your face, trumping in your general direction, jolly good for bringing you down to earth. One thing I have learned is that my “support” map looks very different now to back then, people don’t actually like trouble, and you don’t like to drop it at their door. Load of crap. You overexaggerate your friends network, you have to draw a diagram of how it all works, and The SS say “well that’s great then”, presumably whether you’ve got five friends and family or fifty, another box ticked, and a hugely impressive A1 diagram by the way.

Have I mentioned the checklist? The two column, yes/no, what sort of child would you NOT accept checklist? A different colour, religion, one who is disabled? If disabled, what kind of disabled would you manage with? A child with a squint? Seriously? But you fill it in, and try and be honest and say "it depends on how much…in what way" and so on, even though it galls you. I could never tell some of my friends what I said no to. To be honest I can't even remember, it was another loathesome ticky box, awful looking back, and actually quite ridiculous, since a lot of the things on the list would only become apparent later in a child's life. As indeed we found to our cost not all problems or debilitating issues were on that hateful list.

Point is we were seriously grilled, poked, challenged, researched into. Some of our friends and family were actually interviewed. Everybody knew. Suddenly my cocoon of privacy was invaded. I didn't need privacy any more did I? I had nothing to hide actually, no dark secrets, but I had been used to a bit of a private life. And the jokes went like "if Social Services could see us now…" as we got occasionally drunk and fell over, lost our hats, played air guitar until 3am then stayed in bed until the afternoon at weekends, and generally behaved very irresponsibly, but all in all, innocent fun, the calm before the storm. Actually those things became a massive relief of the pressure of the prolonged probing. My daughter would now say if she were reading this (which she won't be, for a very long long long time, if ever), "mummy look at that alliteration!" And she would also say "mummy, you are sooooooooo embarrassing".

Can I just say at this point, that we were genuinely taking this seriously. We would not have put ourselves through the excruciating interrogation and mind searching if we weren't. And we did do all the research, and more. And we subjected ourselves to everyone's questioning, and suddenly everyone had an opinion about us, it, everything. And we listened, and learned. And as the Sydney Opera House, grown up wallpaper became the most expensive lining paper ever, after I painted it a delightful shade of magnolia I felt we were becoming child friendly, and growing up a bit, and starting to genuinely understand what we might be letting ourselves in for.

There's a point where your "pack", the whole gubbins about you, your life, universe and everything, gets put forward for approval to adopt, and you start waiting (not waiting again I hear you cry?), I'm sure there were timelines, guidelines, I normally have to know these, and I expect I did. And I expect I was rather rancid. Waiting patiently is not my thing. I cannot tell you how long this process took from the first inquisitive phone call, but it was years. On the outside I'm laughing off the wait (it will happen), and the possibility that they might reject us (surely not went the cry), you have so much to give. On the inside it's like I went into the butterfly house at the zoo, and accidentally turned on a leaf blower. I was waiting, for them to say no. "You are not our cup of tea". "We found out something terrible about you". "We will not allow you to adopt a child". "It is not like in your mother in law's day". "Now we have learned lessons, and having done all our comprehensive research on you we find you unsuitable".

But bugger me. All of a sudden they deign to say that you are OK, in fact not just OK, you are great, we approve of you, you are acceptable, suitable, actually all right. Well gee thanks! You are too kind, what a compliment, I am proud to accept your acceptance. I think we're all right too by the way. You just took a while to agree with us.

Celebrate, No, Wait

You celebrate then. Is that premature? Well it bloody doesn't feel it. We did it, we got there, they said we'll do. It's like passing your GCSEs, A Levels, Driving Test, getting engaged, married, whatever, it feels good. And you can start looking. You have permission. Yes dears, I mean you look for children. Might I mention the magazine that you got, with a special membership of Adoption UK, you receive a free magazine. Which is quite interesting, with its articles about adoption "issues", and they have a forum online actually which you can access for free. I have spent days of my life obsessively looking at that flaming forum, because it's full of useful experiences from likeminded people. Though I did realise the problem a while ago, that people don't post when they're in a boring state, only when they're at one extreme, i.e. hugely happy and successful and rightly want to share, or the other, as in completely in the doodoo. Despite this I still look at it now. I know it's bad for me, like that one last wafer thin mint for Mr Creosote (watch and learn on Youtube if you are unfamiliar), but I can't help it.

Anyway their publication also came with a section, only for subscribers, like the classified ads. Full of little pictures of poor little lost lambs, for you to express an interest in. Which you can freely do, but they're all a bit difficult. You see the easy ones are placed by their local authority in the local area, then there are slightly more difficult children who might go out of area, bit of a bigger catchment area, and then, well then The SS struggles. When I say difficult children, I'm not being funny, but older children, sibling groups, disabled, a bit complicated in whatever way. They are the ones who wait longest, sometimes forever. So, they don't encourage you to look at them at first, it might put you off. In reality, they have invested in you and probably want to get a local child or children placed with you.

So at first you start with the local team. They have a list of current and prospective children up for adoption as they say, going through the system to come out the other side ready for adopting. We were actually approved for two children up to six years old. That sounds good doesn't it, definitely must be a large selection of those? Well sorry to disillusion you but apparently not. So, they presented us with a group of three children one of whom was seven (excuse me but how does that fit our approval for two under six?) and a group of two who had family somewhere two minutes away (bit difficult then, probably bump into them regularly, not very sensible), and that basically was that. We should take comfort that they were the only children in the right band needing adopting in our county, shouldn't we? That's what they said, but if you believe that you believe anything.

And we said "so let us go out of county then". Normally you had to wait, I think three months. Why would you do that? If you are approved, and there are no children coming through the system, why would you wait three months when there might be some outside of your little parochial area. This is when we started to learn that these "local" authorities do things their own special way. Each one has their own foibles, good and bad, and make their own minds up about their own policies and practices. Sometimes you're in the right one, sometimes you are crapped on from a great height because you live in the wrong area, and their procedures are different from those of the local authority just a few miles down the road. Anyway at this point we were unaware of the fact that our SS was like a bag of spanners, and went with everything they said, were at their mercy. But they did allow us to seek our new family out of county early, and this was massively exciting and held huge potential. The whole of a region was at our fingertips, we could search a wider area in a different way. And we did. We went to a children exhibition. Literally. From the classified ads, to a child display. A great hall with stands and hundreds of pictures and bumf about children who were up for adoption. You walk around and make notes, and then go and speak to the social workers about which ones you like. Just like a fair or an auction. But you have to play the game don't you? So we expressed interest in just the one lot, a pair, three and four, girl and boy, beautiful, big smiles. Met their foster carer, amazing woman, their social worker, said the right things. You don't get your auction paddles out or anything, but writing your name down, is like leaving a bid. We signed on the line and left. Over lunch we talked about them, looked at their brochure pictures, started to form fantasies about being their parents. That was it, the start of a bit of an obsession. So we informed The SS of our decision, the Custard Cream Social Worker thought it was marvellous, would take it forward and speak to her counterpart in the other place. God, another one. We went back to work hard and play hard, and to wait … some more...

More paperwork, more frustration, more questions, more of everything, but after more of that came something new, and another boom moment. We got selected. We were invited to a panel of judges. Sorry, not judges, just good people. But it did feel like we had got through the preliminary round of Adopters Got Talent. However then it turned out to be like the worst job interview ever. I think five or six or maybe even seven or eight people chosen for their knowledge and expertise, of children and adoption, your life in their hands. Although you get caught up in the whole warm glow of being the chosen ones, and feel like nothing can phase you, it kind of does anyway. Nerves, best Sunday clothes, best accent (I'm a bit northern at times you see). It's presenting yourself, you are the real incarnation of what they have read on paper. But surely if they've read all about you, and you've jumped through all the hoops, how can they reject you on meeting you? As I said, job interview. Actually I don't think you necessarily have to go to this. You might wonder why we did then? The problem is do you let the representative of The SS go in your place? Or no one go and represent you? Whilst these few good citizens make the most important decision about your life for you, so you can sit by the phone waiting to hear, well, that was not an option for us. We were already in other peoples' hands, and this was a part we needed to be in control of as much as possible. Due to our amazing performance on that day, bit of yodelling, a tap dance, and a modern interpretation of the nutcracker, all the judges lit their lights for us. We were approved, matched, whatever you want to call it. And were on cloud nine, or is there a ten? As we drove off in our two-seater while we waited for the feedback just to make sure, we didn't know whether it was soon to be relegated for the more sensible family size option. We got the call from The SS a bit later, and spent the rest of the day kind of in shock, and kind of scared, and just a wee bit proud of ourselves. And put the two-seater car on Ebay.

Guess what we did then? Right answer. Waited. Just a little few more tenterhooks to be hung on. Don't forget at this point we hadn't seen the children who we were going to parent, in real life. We assumed they did really exist, but we could only take The SS's word for it. In your head they are suddenly yours, and so you can start sorting your house, their room, telling people, wandering round toyshops or the children's clothing aisles without feeling like some fraud or weirdo. We told Dog. She raised a furry eyebrow, decided she was OK about it, and ate another plantpot.

Caravan Of Love

Unfortunately the handover / takeover (sorry, I can't think of another expression) from foster carers to us was a bit delayed because the Social Worker was on holiday. Now I know Social Workers are human, but seriously, let's make the children wait some more while she goes skiing?! Apparently no-one else could do her job. When she returned from St Moritz or Verbiers, the plan was formed, not by us, but for us. Don't forget our lives were now completely under the control of The SS, and we vud do vot zey said. Because the children were out of our area, they were going to put us up for a few days, so the children could visit us locally, which was really lovely of them, and hugely appreciated. They chose a caravan, at the end of a wintry February.

I have never stayed in a caravan, I'm not posh or anything, but this idea I found slightly peculiar, and it caused all sorts of visions in my head like those showers that were also a loo, and it tipping up if we both stood on one side. Silly me, it was static and didn't have visible wheels so nothing to worry about. The only thing was it was winter and bloody Baltic out there… Still the holiday camp it was placed in had some good chips, and tuppence machines to while away the hours on my birthday which happened whilst we were there. Great. Oh and I might have taken a bottle of wine or two. And can you believe it had heating, well of sorts. Dog had a holiday in kennels. We missed her. But the good news is she spends so much time chatting to other canines whilst there, she always loses her voice, and does have a marvellous time. I have to say looking back it wasn't exactly normal. I was told the other day that a two-week introduction schedule is normal. And they would normally visit you in your own home, sorry their future home, so this caravan business for a few days was a bit off the wall, but as usual you go along with it. Ain't going to be no spanners in no works for us.

I can't tell you how nervous we were on the day we met the children. So many questions, we almost couldn't speak. What if they run away / don't like us / scream / we drop one … those kind of things. I had never actually been responsible for a small person, their parents have always been hovering somewhere, and we have always played the naughty and ever so eccentric Auntie and Uncle, buying inappropriate gifts like drum kits because it's funny, and plopping them head first into Granddad's pond. I mean what do you talk about with a three year old?

We got to the Wunderbar Foster Carers house and the door opened. There they were on the doorstep, Girl a bit shy (the first and last time this ever happened), Boy more forward, he started leaping up and down and she followed his lead. And we went in. They had seen our photos. We had prepared each of them a book, with photos of us and our life, and tried to take them on a journey through Dog's eyes. After all she was adopted too, and it was her house, and they were coming to live with her. So they already knew us as "mummy and daddy", we thought we might grow into those names, but that was a strange thing to hear. It didn't mean anything to them, but we hoped in time it would. I remember feeling overwhelmingly flattered. Thinking that these little beings would eventually consider that we had earned those titles.

So under the very watchful eye of their Social Worker, who was very very very very very fond of them (can I stress that some more?) we had our first meeting with these little beings who were going to be ours. They were the first children this Social Worker had removed from their birth parents and my goodness she was very very very very very attached to them. The foster carer, the amazing one (I do mean this, she was a wonderful lady) was there too of course, we played games in the kitchen and then said goodbye to come back the next day. And slightly speechless, which if you knew us would come as rather a surprise, neither of us being backwards at coming forwards, we went and had a glass of that wine. I guess by the end of our few days there, the children thought we lived in a small box on a campsite. Probably a bit confusing for the poor things when they were driven half way across the country to a bricks and mortar place. Bit bloody confusing for all of us really.

The few days in the caravan was interesting looking back, we were sort of learning what to do with children, it was all very false and we felt like we'd stolen them when we were allowed out together. But we also felt like, to an outsider, we were just a family (at last). One not so good memory of a 45 minute meltdown by Boy over snakes and ladders persists, we didn't know what to do to soothe him. Of course we'd had the training, but we couldn't understand why it was happening because we didn't know him. And no one told us he always did that, until afterwards. Still whatever, we sort of laughed about it later. What a joyous time we had, we went for picnics, on steam trains, bouncy places, Harvesters Restaurant, gave them baths, read to them, watched cartoons. All the things you wish that you could do as an adult but unless you have kids you're not allowed. We acted the part, and so did they. It went well. All our friends knew what we were doing, waiting for us to come back and report. So it had to go well really. After all this we said farewell, and came home to the brick house without any wheels. In the day we had before they joined us, it was panic stations. I told you we still hadn't finished the house... Well that day the kitchen floor went down, entire contents of the spare room went in the attic, not a speck of dust lived to fight another day, well that lasted a few months anyway. It was like a health and safety inspection. We were exhausted, and then the next day they arrived, meeting a rather disgruntled Dog, who always bears a grudge about coming home from kennels, and if she hadn't already lost her voice from barking, wouldn't be speaking to us. The children were rather scarily not just visiting. They were here to stay, forever. The lovely foster carers brought them and their stuff. This was my home, so I was in charge, but it didn't feel like it. Weird. But it was OK, they went to their bunk bed that night beautifully. They had a room each, but we put them in the same one, with everything as close to how it was in their foster home, same bedding, same toys, so they would feel OK. So, this was now our family, and was how it would be forever. This was big, BIG big.

Next day we met the foster carers, dressed as pirates… the children, not the foster carers …don't ask. We had an enormous breakfast, good grief they ate a lot, again the children, not the foster carers. The children liked eating. In fact given the chance they would not stop. Even now this happens. I lost count of how many times I heard "I hungry" in those early days. Apparently this was them vocalising worry, not knowing why they feel funny, or what could help, so turning to something physical, satisfying… food. Actually a lot of the time all they needed was reassurance, to feel safe. But still, food was good too, we introduced them to our rather overstocked pantry (my hoarding obsession has taken over in there) not long after, to show them that there would always be food. After said big pirate breakfast we, they, said goodbye to the foster carers, who drove off into the distance, leaving us on our own. No backup, no more answers, just us and the children, just this new family. We were scared I suppose, but couldn't show that. Be confident. You are parents now. You are the adults. They ran blooming rings round us. But they were ours, Our Boy and Our Girl.

Ceilings Are For Bouncing Off

So many people who have talked about us, have said that because we were from a Services background, that would be superb, because clearly we would be good with routines and sensible, which is what seemed to have worked in really helping these children make progress. Coming from utter and absolute chaos and devastation into a life of knowns, and structure had brought them up to speed. And this was very true. They were basically feral when they first came into care, and in 18 months had learned to speak, sit at a table and eat, rather than off the floor, be polite, and well, just be a bit more "normal", or socially acceptable, there was a bed time, a wake up time, breakfast, snack, lunch, snack, tea, snack, bath, tv, bed. Sorted. It worked, and we felt we could carry this on, and this was really important, because then their daily lives were not changing, just the people in it. May I say though, this is nothing to do with being Services. Do you bring your work home with you? No, neither did we. We loved the organised work life, but when released we did our own thing.

We liked life, colour, noise, surprises, being different. But nevertheless we stuck at it. We learned the routines. I had made a freezer full of child food, spag bol, macaroni cheese, shepherd's pie. How sensible was that? We cleaned up wee and poo, changed sheets, tidied up, listened, interacted, bought velvety car seats, dispensed words of wisdom, mopped up tears, laughed, cried, and generally spent every ounce of energy doing the right things. Dog? She was a bit nonplussed to be fair. All of a sudden these small people were bugging her, following her, over stroking, demanding her attention not always as nicely as she needed, and they were want, want, want. She did a lot of hiding. And perfected the art of looking displaced, downtrodden, and generally disappointed. I hope I am not projecting here. But I must admit at times I also wished I could hide from these three and four year old whirling dervishes. Just for five minutes.

You're told to take time, to block out the outside world, to calm everyone down, no visitors, no presents, just bonding. Which is good, but god the time did not fly. It wasn't normal and normal is what we all needed. But we followed the words of wisdom, we avoided everyone else, family, friends, for I guess three weeks. We spent all our time forming a unit. Talk about intense.

Desperate new grandparents tried their hardest not to put pressure on. But they deserved a peek. So we Skyped. Oh, the wonders of modern technology. That became the reality for the children for a bit, grandparents who they had seen pictures of, suddenly talking to them on a screen. The children were OK with this, they did little speaky parts, when they could sit there for long enough, they were only three and four after all. And that was very exciting. Involved a lot of explaining. If you can explain a family construction to a child that has no memory of what that meant. And then came the visitation rota. So one set of grandparents at a time they were allowed to visit. They had to stay, because they lived 100s of miles away, and the moment they walked through the door they were pounced upon, and responded by giving. Time, energy, stuff. They were great, for a couple of days. They had advice, knowledge, patience. It kind of helped. And then they left. Which also helped, sorry mother, and mother in law.

I haven't really told you about how the children really reacted to this strange world they had been plopped into. They were certainly lively. They were excited, agitated, played us off against each other, tested us, would we or wouldn't we? They argued, fought, shouted, laughed, burped, challenged, might have slept a bit, bounced, crashed, broke things, bashed things, laughed some more. Basically they adjusted, on the surface, amazingly. They fell into this new existence, like it was natural, and just expected us to know what to do. Fair enough. Looking back, I don't think we thought anything was odd, unusual, unexpected. At the end of the day it was all frigging bonkers wasn't it? And we had no benchmark so we wouldn't know whether anything was awry. So it wasn't. She was chirpy, big eyed, observant, bright, blonde and beautiful. He was smart, canny, edgy, handsome, cute. She wound him up, he reacted, he hit the roof, so did she. He overdid the physical affection, would put his arms round your neck so tight steam came out of your ears. Especially if you were a bloke. She wouldn't leave your side, or if she did she was with him. Where he was, she was. They were together, a pair, inseparably ever present, until the explosion. Then she was with us. Then they were back, weirdly together. We began to feel tremendous love for these funny little people.

We had decided that they should start nursery and school as soon as possible, so that they would understand that life wasn't just spent within four walls, and so they might socialise with other small people. I'd done the rounds, I didn't realise at that time that in all reality I had jumped any queue for a place that had invisibly formed, and my children rose above others, because they were "looked after". I just thought how nice everyone was, and was riding high at my success in impressing people and getting them to agree that they needed my children to attend their establishment. I did tell the relevant people originally, that I had no idea what the children were like as I hadn't met them yet. But when I turned up with them no one else knew that, so that was good. As far as other parents were concerned these were our children, no one looked at us like we were naïve, new to this, felt like kidnappers, scared shitless. And the children both settled into their respective institutions, and made their presence felt immediately. The teachers couldn't believe it really, and neither could we.

I then didn't know what to do with myself, I was on adoption leave from work, and I'd never had this sort of time on my hands, so I busied myself becoming domesticated. That has worn off by the way. I am one of those whose sock collection has lots of half pairs, and whose Tupperware box assortment is mighty impressive in its lidlessness. I now have magnificent dust, and realise that you see cobwebs more when they are dusty, and my laundry basket has one gold lamé thing that has taken up residence (which is not mine or Hub's to my knowledge). But at that time my domesticity knew no bounds. Of course I only had five hours a day, in school time, and I didn't know any other parents, and what do you do all shagging day anyway. I've never been one for daytime telly. Although I could see why you could be. I actually have no idea what I spent my time doing. Certainly nothing constructive apart from cleaning and washing. Why didn't I learn mandarin, or tidy the attic, or do good charity work? I have no idea. I did take a little job in a café, which meant at least I was talking to grown up humans.

At this point I had told my school that I couldn't come back from adoption leave. There was no way I could be there for the children at school drop off and pick up whilst working there, and it wouldn't be right to entrust them to someone else, they needed us, we needed to be the ones they looked to, and to know we would be there. The only thing I can say in my defence is that when I had got the children to nursery or school, actually dressed and having had a wholesome breakfast (something different every day) with all their gubbins, I felt like I had achieved something, and was so cream crackered I couldn't think, and I then only had five hours, only five hours to regroup, five hours that felt like five minutes, before I set off on my walk across town to pick up one, who would be camouflaged, if the background was a Picasso, in paint, food, having wet herself, bruised herself, broken something, and would hide every time I walked in. Then back across town to the other, who would have ripped, lost or chewed his clothes, and would also be covered in food, paint and dirt, to walk home, to entertain and be entertained, feed, water, and care for them for the next two to three hours before Hub got home, cream crackered himself, by which time he had generally received 42 annoying text messages from me to describe the antics that had gone on.

We held our first child's birthday party. I guess we both had memories of our own jolly parties as children. All those memories of your own childhood that you have held on to, which made you who you are. I remember a pink and white party, everyone had to come in those colours, all the food was pink, or white. I don't know why. But there was definitely pink custard. Why don't we get that now. Pink custard is a life necessity. And my friend broke her toe. I remember ice cream cakes, and cookies bigger than your head. I remember skating in my wellies on the frozen flooded river. My brother and I screeched and our bellies hurt from laughing. I tripped over a twig, and broke my nose. He shoved an icicle up it. My nose is still wonky. I remember climbing up the haystacks in the local farm and jumping off the top down the hole in the middle. You would go slowly and then shoot downwards like a rocket. My friend broke her leg.

Not everything got broken, but it was haphazard, and that was how life should be, you didn't worry about anything, no cares crept up on you. I remember my Great Aunt spilling tea on herself on our Cornish picnic, and taking her big red bloomers off to dry in the sun. I remember mum hiding our dinner in the coal bunker in a treasure hunt. I remember kicking off my shoe dancing in the garden and it landing in a tree never to be seen again, I was in such trouble. I remember my brother getting a fishing hook stuck in his hand instead of in a crab, stupid boy. I remember making pressed flowers and Nessie hunting. All those things made me. And this is what we dreamed of for our own children. We wanted them to have that kind of existence. Not the broken limbs necessarily, but climbing trees, laughing, bouncing, eating jelly and pink not yellow custard, and dancing. So our first party was a nerve-wracking experience. Boy didn't know any other children. So I asked the teacher to pick some, and I wrote to their parents. five came, and we had a pirate party (yes, we did all loved pirates). I had a wicked eye patch, the dog had a neckerchief. I was such a cool mum (told you I like fancy dress). And we had jelly and custard (albeit yellow). This was good. This was how it was meant to be.

Family continued to come to visit. The children bounced off the ceilings for the entire time and were showered with gifts and attention. Friends came, the children were showered with gifts, and attention. They didn't really understand the strange transition they were in, so we talked and played suitable therapeutic games, and analysed everything and tried to remember all our Dan Brown readings (he's a guru by the way, not Dan Brown of The Da Vinci Code although much of what the guy says is a bit mysterious. No, the other academic one). We found out the importance of boundaries, routine and structure, the lovingly given gifts got broken, but things seemed good. Dog reluctantly came to accept that she had some more members of the pack to put up with. Bless her, she got mercilessly teased on occasions, and still came back for more. She was intrigued at first by these two new small animals, but then I think it developed into boredom, her having the concentration of a goldfish, unless there is a biscuit which she is not allowed to have, in which case she will enter a staring competition with it. The biscuit usually wins by the way.

There's a statutory duty for Social Services to check up on you every four to six weeks before you officially adopt, because actually the children are classed as "in care". Fortunately the young, keen, slightly obsessed Social Worker, remember the one who was very very very very very fond, seemed to find it too difficult to drive for an hour (imagine that… a whole hour), to visit so we were able to get our former Posh Social Worker to come instead. I must explain at this point that the children have a social worker, and you have one too. Not the same one who you went through the process with but a new one. We had the old one as a new one if you see what I mean. Remember the one who we really liked, and still do. The posh one with the amusing approach to the gogglebox as a form of childcare.

When our boy decided he was changing his name (yes you read me right, that is what he unequivocally decided) … she was the one we called upon to talk to him. We didn't want to fall into the category of middle class do gooders changing a child's name from Hero to Jack, or

Prosecco to Poppy. She popped over, and I left her there, for an hour. By the time I returned, all my homemade lemon drizzle which was supposed to be going camping with us, had mysteriously disappeared, and she was categoric that it was what he wanted, the lemon drizzle and the name change. He was adamant. So that's what we did from that day forward, on her advice. We did what he seemed to desperately want, and called him by his new name. All his cousins accepted it straight away, as did his sister, who went from trumpeting his original name across the playground when we went to get him every day, to using his new one even louder. He was very proud of himself for this. So we were OK with it too. In hindsight we probably shouldn't have been, we may have questioned his motivations more, but we had sought expert advice and acted on it. He still keeps that name today. There is no mention of his previous existence, his former self, he was completely reinvented at that point, in his own head. He was five years old. How is that possible? But he did it, and now nobody seems to remember the boy who came before. Nobody mentions the name. When I see it written on a document even I have to check myself. And it reminds me of the confusions and uncertainties of the time, and the desire to get things right, and heaps on the guilt again that things even then had potential to go so badly wrong. The indicators were there, we just didn't see them, but then no-one else did, and they were experts.

Our parents were besotted. We had brought these beautiful little children into their lives and they needed their love. It came in spades. OK so they had not held them in their arms as new born babies, and the children were opinionated little sods, but they fell in love. And our children learned what grandparents were for. Well, they learned that grandparents would let you do everything your parents didn't. And this meant they were all right. They were cuddlers, and grandparents love that don't they? It was weird really. We would see an immediate shift in affection from us to them, or anyone else who happened to be around to be honest. Boy was still absolutely indiscriminate. He would turn his back on us and go for the nearest adult. It was strange, but we reassured ourselves that he was embracing all this new family and protecting or asserting his place. He would stop talking to us, or listening, and would rather go and hold anyone else's hand but ours. I did feel a bit sorry about this. I compared it, inevitably to my sister and brother in laws interactions with their children, but had to tell myself that this was the new normal, and that is just how it was, and that it was good that he liked our whole family.

Boy learned to read, he was definitely keen as mustard at school, and did so amazingly well. I was very proud of him He was bright. Girl was so observant, and followed his lead a lot. When it came time for her to bring books home from school she remembered how he had learned phonetically, which was fab, except the first books they get have no actual words, so she made them up and pronounced the made up words phonetically anyway. "Kuh Ah Tuh … Cat". We listened intently struggling to contain our amusement. They were both incredibly loud, and we realised that they wound each other up, and then basically exploded, a lot. Thinking about it, it was ridiculously hard, on both of us. We didn't know what was right and wrong, what was normal what not, what was to be expected, or what we should worry about. Yes, I know, just like any new parent, but what we struggled with was the unknowns from the time before us, and there was no run in. That was invisible baggage. It didn't help that nobody seemed to really know what it looked like, what had actually happened to the children at the beginning of their lives. This is when the advice started coming thick and fast. All children do that, that's normal, you're over cautious / protective / concerned. Whatever we said there was always an answer, so we cracked on.

We were seeing a therapist (this is usual by the way, we weren't nuts back then). Just for us, to allow us to talk about the children and us. Which was amazingly helpful, and we had eight sessions funded by The SS, arranged by the nice Social Worker, with the custard cream problem. She was quite forward thinking really, as we would never have asked for this support ourselves. The therapist recommended we should have more sessions as she saw we struggled with the foibles of this new life, and as we got to know the children a little better. It was like the supervision that you get if you are in a stressful medical or social care type job, or indeed a Social Worker. Sadly the response from The SS was deafening in its silence. Now I couldn't possibly say that when The SS places a child outside its own area, the child is out of sight, out of mind, and let's not talk about the financial savings made but looking back over the notes, the authority to do things was only delegated to our SS, the funding still was the responsibility of the original authority, for three years, after adoption, so they should have been more involved. The lack of response at that time just meant we carried on. You would wouldn't you? You have no choice. There are little children at the centre, and you can't just stop and put them down for a bit. We didn't really need the therapy or help did we? We could just do it couldn't we? We didn't complain or make a fuss, well not publicly, and nobody pushed for us to get help. Our therapist was frustrated for us, but there was not a lot she could do, and she had a huge caseload already, so we left it there, and the status quo became the norm.

Remember at this time, and probably for around ten months The SS continued with the statutory visits, and to be honest we were so fed up of being under scrutiny however nice Posh Social Worker was, that we just wanted to be normal, and actually adopt them which would make these bloody outsiders go away. The adoption order came through and we were quietly overjoyed. Looking back we should have realised that even ten months seems hasty, but that's with hindsight. We had our day in court with a proper judge (no wig sadly). When about twenty of us filed in to the Courtroom his face was an absolute picture! What a day. All the family came, all the friends, all went to court on a jolly old train, with a picnic on the way, which we shared with fellow passengers to their bemusement. We had a party, with a proper balloon man, a big cake, jelly, custard (yellow) and everything! Everyone was overjoyed, and so full of hope.

A New Normal

I suppose we had started to see some different behaviours back then but there were bound to be ups and downs, so we tried not to overly worry, people kept telling us all kids were like that. And the more challenging part of a character is what we felt we could deal with, and why we were chosen. But the mood swings had become evident, tantrums had began to gain momentum, the animalistic howls echoing probably halfway down the road. We started to notice a change in Boy's outbursts, any little thing could set him off, and the wailing that ensued could break glass. Nothing could calm him or console him. Like that first time in the caravan. Except if you asked him a question, or made a statement which didn't fit the situation. He would stop dead in his tracks, stop screaming and in five seconds be nice as pie. Which when it started we thought it was a little shall I say, different, but as time went on, and you'd hear it start, like an air raid siren, warning you of what was to come, it was more than unusual, it was plain worrying. What on earth must be going on for him to make him react like that? It was like looking at a picture of pain, like that Scream by Edvard Munch.

We also realised that he had an absolute inability to do anything but win. Yes, I know, normal. If he didn't there would be an outburst as described. As far as he was concerned he was going to win everything, he came across as so confident in his own ability, that people got sucked in and he was so charismatic and believable. I know it sounds like something that other children experience, but this was so extreme, that you couldn't really play a game. We persevered to try and help him to become accustomed to "not winning", and modelled behaviour to him. Laugh when you lose, shake someone's hand, think of the fun we had. And he wanted to play. So you were caught, if you didn't feel like giving a lesson in fair play, because you knew it would lead to the inevitable rage, or gloating so that Girl would cry and an argument would ensue, so you would face the tantrum anyway, because you wouldn't play. Catch 22. The jealousy of others, particularly his sister made it so difficult to praise or reward anyone else, as it would lead to a slough of despond and put a dampener on any positive situation.

His hyperactiveness knew no bounds. Given any small trigger he would bounce off all four walls and the roof, no matter where he was or what or who was in his way, he had no method of self-regulation and no consciousness of socially acceptable norms. Dog knew. She hid under the table, a lot, and made herself very small, scaredy-dog was her new norm. He was hypervigilant. Nothing went unnoticed, even though he didn't appear to be listening, he heard everything, and wanted to hear, as if paranoid he would sneak behind doors, to the top of the stairs in the middle of the night, listen through walls to see what was going on, were you talking about him, was he missing out? He made hugely inappropriate attachments, if he was in public he would approach anybody and start chatting, we realised that the problem with this was that nobody can refuse to talk to a polite little boy, and encouraged by that he would then not leave them alone.

The purple rinse grannies at family do's would be captivated by this smart little fellow with his shirt and tie on. He would eventually be reined in to try to encourage him to play with other children but it would never go as well as discussing the dahlias with Great Aunt Deirdre. He would claim to have made some new best friends, even if he had only walked past a group of children, they were his best buddies. Our parents commented on it. They looked after him on occasion and found they were constantly on edge, because he would just go and disappear. And so unbeknown to us they would draft in reinforcements to help them. They always said yes, of course they would look after the children, but then the plan would be put in place, so that there were rare occasions when they needed to be alone with him. I only know this now. And I am upset. I thought it was because everybody wanted to see the children, and I find it was for our parents protection… oh dear.

And the lying… my word…the lying. That phrase about arguing black is white sums it up. So something would happen and you would "wonder" how, why, who and even if you made it clear you had seen it happen or went to great lengths to explain how you knew, he would deny knowledge, responsibility or even being there. The best thing was not to ask, but then again how does a child learn right and wrong. A proper conundrum. If there were bite marks in the bed, he hadn't slept in it. When the heating, which he was not allowed to touch, was turned up to scorching, he was in a different room, he didn't know how to do it. Remember he was only five or six years old. It was incredible.

These are just snippets of his behaviour which began to impact so much on our daily lives. It was draining, because we were always trying to do the right thing, whilst being completely normal too, and to parent Girl too, who we now realise was becoming increasingly withdrawn and overlooked. Not a day would pass without some explosion, or air raid warning, and then the fall out from it afterwards. Trying to help him in some way come to terms with his feelings. Dealing with him started to take the majority of our time. We always say he probably had about 80% of our attention, where Girl got 20%. There was no down time. When he was in bed all we did was try to analyse the situation. God we must have been so boring. But you couldn't stop. You had to think of the long term gain, for him at least. We had opened our hearts and allowed ourselves to fall in love with him, and now the instinct to protect kicked in.

We persevered, of course we did, this was our new normal. We were as normal as blueberry pie! So, we had dreamed of it before, and we finally managed to take the children skiing in a foreign place. They were amazing, both so natural. We put them in ski school with lots of other children for the ultimate experience. But it didn't feel right. Boy would wander off, go missing. He refused to listen to the instructor. He was only little and we couldn't ensure his safety. We also stayed in our favourite family hotel where we had been going for a decade. And he went ballistic, he screamed, he wet the bed, he had tantrums, he could not cope. We went twice in two years, and the second time, when he felt he could ski like Franz Klammer, he would just go off and over the edge. He just absolutely refused not to. Giving this responsibility to the poor young ski dudes made us feel terribly guilty. It was also downright dangerous. The other delightful memory of this occasion was the screaming.

On this holiday he had such a dickie fit over breakfast, I carried him out of the breakfast room and up the stairs, as a bloody heavy six year old. Kicking and screaming all the way, him that is, not me. We didn't know why it started, but it definitely did. I left our poor companions in shock pondering what just happened over their abundance of boiled eggs. On that same hollibob, on the way back we had to take the ferry, where usually we tunnelled under the sea, because it was quick. It did not go well. He was beside himself for some reason, he screamed, and stropped, and then sat under the table, and refused to let go of the table leg, where he stayed for a lot of the journey. Girl at this point pretended this was not happening and ate lunch, and played with her computer game. All eyes were on us from other passengers. What were we doing to this poor boy? And we almost began to think this too. What were we doing, that was so bad?

He wanted to do things, but when we arranged it, or it came to pass, he would go to pieces. It was the same with special days, Christmas, Easter, birthdays, he would get to the moment, not be able to handle it and so then it didn't meet his expectations and he was disappointed, then just spoil it, for himself and consequently for anyone around him. If he had the chance to do something new, like ride a bike, and it was a slight challenge, he would fling things around, including himself scream, kick anything in range, and generally protest. He threw his bike across the park, and kicked it so hard I thought he would break himself, and then blamed the bike for attacking his shin. He then kicked the car, because his bike had hurt him.

One time, we went to the local music shop and he chose an instrument. We arranged lessons, and he was unbelievably good. He had such an ear for music, still does, making my foray with the funny little instrument, that I pretend to play with my fellow weirdo YouTubers, look like some five year old's school performance. This was great, finally not everyone in our family was tone deaf. But when he owned this yearned-for instrument, he did not want to play it. If you mentioned it he would get angry, then tantrums a gogo. He "misplaced" his lesson book, in fact as far as he was concerned it never existed.

He joined Beavers, but he wasn't interested in the challenges, he didn't do well with the others. We took him to swimming every week, but he messed around in the pool so much it was dangerous for him and for the other children and they kept telling me, a bit like the ski instructors, that I needed to have a word or not come back. He was good though, he could swim, he just didn't seem to want to. I kept taking him. Believe you me there are other things I would rather have been doing, that being boiled alive in the viewing area at the swimming baths, but we wanted him to have the opportunity, and I would be there to see him. He then went swimming with school. They had the same problem. Unfortunately they also had 29 other children to watch over. It did not go well. I got spoken to, again.

I had one of those birthdays. That ends in a zero. I was sort of looking forward to it, and sort of not. I hadn't quite got over my last zero birthday a decade before. When the day finally arrived, we had arranged a very rare and flipping expensive baby sitter, and planned to go to our favourite restaurant, nothing OTT, I was a responsible human being now. On the day I was showered with gifts, a mini bottle of champagne with a straw, a box of violet creams, and a new number plate for my car to remind me of my advancing years. I was very special that day. On that day also, my boy had an indescribable meltdown. It lasted from the moment he got up to… well later. We did not go out, Hub took Girl, and the baby sitter to McDonalds. I stayed at home, lay in Girl's bed and listened to the screaming.

People cannot understand now, why we can definitely say that my Xti'ith birthday was a date we could put our finger on to say that something was wrong, but if whenever you looked at your car you remembered lying weeping because your child wouldn't stop, then you might remember it too. I jumped out of a plane around then too. With a parachute you understand. This was another bucket list gift from a wonderful person. I was so excited. I did it strapped to a red devil (handsome devil at that). And despite feeling sick for two hours afterwards, I was elated. In a kind of I have landed, strapped to a handsome chap, after falling out of the sky type of way. The kind of thing that changes peoples' perceptions on life, because they realise how small and insignificant their little bit of the world is, compared to the big and beautiful sky they have just fallen through. I was so proud of myself (despite the trying not to vomit bit) until my child standing on the ground did not want to speak to me, and belittled it, and just took the piss (which seemed really odd for such a little boy, and which brought me back down to earth quicker than any falling out of an aircraft could).

We tried to find methods for motivation. We tried star charts. We tried long-term earning opportunities, or short-term reward, to no avail. He couldn't think longer than the moment he was in. That was fruitless. We tried instant win options, who doesn't love an immediate reward? But consequences either good or bad meant nothing. This made it so hard to get him to understand right from wrong, because the end didn't matter. Big things in life, achievements, were hard fought, for all of us. We wanted him to succeed, because if he didn't that was like the end of the world. But these struggles extended to each and every little aspect of life as well. From getting up in the morning to going to bed, life was a struggle. Boy wanted to win at everything, brushing his teeth, eating cornflakes, getting dressed, not getting dressed, drinking, not drinking, the basics of life, he had to be first, the one and only. His sister was mainly an obstacle to progress. Until he needed her. And as she grew up a bit, she didn't need him any more. She was no longer scared of him, she stopped making herself small and hiding like Dog, and she began to assert herself. Oh my word did she. Bolshy madam. Which caused more friction than ever.

The point is that life's about some you win some you lose, and I guess we all try to instil in our children the sense of fair play, and work hard to achieve your goal, stick at it. Eventually you hope that this works, that they will prove to themselves that sometimes it's fun to just have a go. That parents are not complete fibbers, and the horseshit about applauding other peoples' success, is actually a valid point and can also make you feel good, because then it is possible to not win, and to celebrate someone else's success. In Boy's case, this was a neverending, no glimmers struggle. In his mind, the world was against him, and he would be victorious against the world. Which is probably why he wouldn't do something he found at all challenging, as this would show his Achilles heel. This would mean his defences would be down, and someone might hurt him. So he then stopped doing anything. Our little boy was troubled and we were so worried for him.

Incommunicado-agogo

I want to talk about rejection. Well I don't actually, but I need to. When you are being rejected, it is either blatant. As in the "I don't want you" kind, or it can be more subtle. Along with the "I want to do it", "I don't want to do it", tantrums, and destruction, I had been experiencing both kinds from Boy for over a year I guess. The first time a child says "you are not my mother", you laugh and tell people. It seems bizarrely reassuring. A child who feels confident that saying that will not cause you to turn and run away, must really know that you are not going anywhere. Yes! But when they start saying at seven years old, how much they don't want to be part of the family on a regular basis (when I say regular, I mean daily) it gets a bit hurtful. You try to empathise and understand. The more subtle rejection is what gets to you. So if every time you ask a child to do something they do the opposite, or nothing, or do it and then destroy something, every time someone else is around, you no longer exist, from breakfast time to bedtime your seven year old says not one word to you, I don't suppose you believe that possible? But it happens. I couldn't touch him, even if he came near enough for me to try. I was screamed and raged at (when he was talking to me) pushed, kicked (by accident).

A lot happened when it was just me, and it was just me quite a lot. It was like I was to blame for everything. He wouldn't even look at me. We tried to show him that we loved him unconditionally. We knew that this was a classic manifestation of attachment issues. Try living with it though. I had Girl too. She was not like this. She was a royal pain in the arse at times (I say was.. sorry darling, but still is), but she never rejected us. Or him. But somehow I had to nurture and protect them both. I researched. Words have been bandied around like Child Specific Blocked Care and PTSD. Whatever. The point is whilst this was going on there was no fecking help. We had failed to get further sessions with the therapist, because no one would speak to us, or her, to try to arrange it. We had adopted legally now, so we had no contact with anyone from The SS any more. We should have been careful what we wished for. The day you adopt and they disappear is great, but then it's just you. And Mr Google of course. He is always there. I did look, and thought about our training, and it became apparent that these things are actually quite prevalent in adoptive families.

There is so much research into how trauma in early life, even neo-natal can affect you.

Boy was unquestionably traumatised, and had so much going on in him and for him, that had begun to concern us deeply, and actually trying to parent both children therapeutically with no external guidance or help started to get on top of us, so finally we decided to ask for some external support. I knew that the post-adoption service of The SS existed, wasn't quite sure how to access it, and to be truthful had had my fill of social workers, but by then we had to do something. It felt like we were not coping very well with the deteriorating behaviour, and he seemed so in need of help. Having admitted this to ourselves, and realising that an outside view might help, we had to swallow our pride and admit it to someone else. A bit like the request for extension of our own therapy sessions, I went to the original authority, and had the usual response, i.e. nothing. I went to the reliable Posh Social Worker who tried to find out who to go to, but by then it was the Summer holiday and we all know what that means… Radio silence. Did you know nothing goes wrong at weekends and during holidays?

We had what we thought was the worst Summer on record with escalating behaviour. It does sound contradictory when I read what I just wrote. Behaviour that deteriorated and escalated. It was so confusing, you never knew which Boy you would get from one minute to the next. We did the normal stuff. Went on holiday, Grandparents came, and Granny finally witnessed the full blown screaming habdabs. I think she thought we were exaggerating, until she saw it. Talk about mindblowing. Granny who had only retired as a deputy head a few years before, been a SENCo, and adopted several children, had never seen anything like it. She just couldn't believe it. What a jolly fecking time we all had. Dog rolled in cowshit, consequently turned green, and generally did her own thing.

We all tried our therapeuticness. Well not Dog obviously. And not Girl. She just rolled her eyes, and revelled in the fact that when Boy was doing his thing, she got attention to make up for it, as we desperately tried for it not to affect her. She had her own foibles, but they probably went slightly overlooked, for which we reap the benefits now, but in general she cracked on. She was like a moth to a flame though. When he was not screaming she would seek him out, prod, poke, and then the arguments would start and she would go about her business, leaving the trail of destruction in her wake.

They talk about a trauma bond. I didn't really understand that before, but I realised that when you have been in a place where you are fighting for survival and there is someone else in the same position, whether you like it or not you have a link, an undeniable bond that you can't describe, explain or justify, but it holds you together. We just held out for September when school started again, when we could share our experience with someone. Just needed to get there, without busting a blood vessel. Dog didn't know about time passing. Another being living in the moment. The screaming horrible moment. She rolled in more shit, and then hid.

I carried on doing my "is there anybody there…?" trick, with The SS, and was finally given the name of The mysterious "Lady in the Right Team", so I sent her a direct message.

School term began. I breathed a sigh of relief, as did many parents probably. But they may have had a slightly more fun filled vacation… Finally I could have some time in the day, when I was not required to suppress my human instinct to hide, and I could try to remember who I was and get back some energy. Safe in the knowledge that Boy was in a good place, a known place, a place that he found routine, and loved. After a mere week back at school, we were called in to see the Headmaster. For feck's sake, this was not a good start.

Normally it was only the teacher. This was Mr Boss Man. Turns out it was due to Boy doing something extremely inappropriate during a lesson. Yes peeps, he exposed himself. Pulled his trouser pockets out and walked into class as an elephant if you get my drift. The Head was brilliant, but he did say that if there was a recurrence of this sort of thing (and under normal circumstances) he would have to report our situation to Social Services. I said it's OK, I already have. Now I was not going to take no for an answer. For Christ's sake I didn't want the spectre of anything sexual entering into this mele. That's what the Head was saying really. This boy needed more help than we knew how to give, and we damned well were going to get it. I started emailing and phoning with gusto, and eventually got a response. The "Lady in the Right Team" finally emailed me, asking me who this boy was because she couldn't find any details about him. Excuse me? He is actually one of yours, I distinctly remember spending a few days in your delightful county a couple of years ago, in a caravan, when you deigned to hand him over to me. Another week passed and I sent a reminder email. We are still here you know … have you found him in your files yet…the crisis is ongoing? Hello? Hello? Hello? Is there anybody there? At this point school decided to act. I discovered what a SENCo was. And the one at this school was and remains amazing. I don't know if I have ever met such a genuinely compassionate, and caring individual, with mountains of experience, and so sensible, with a wicked sense of humour. She was a blessed relief in a confusing state of chaos. What a package.

I also took Boy to the GP (recommended by the School, hoping to get a referral to the Child and Adolescent Mental Health Team (CAMHS)). We all thought that this might be the key to unpicking what was happening in his head, what had emerged for him, to try to get some help for him. None of us actually knew anything concrete, we all had our theories, which we discussed at length, but we were all just fumbling around. The School thought that in their experience of children, that his issues might suggest some underlying problem, for which the GP was normally the first point of call to access support. Such a shame though, at the same time that I had an email from The SS to say that they had found out who Boy actually was, and that we could access this Post Adoption support, I was also informed there was a waiting list for this mysterious panacea, as they were short staffed. Oh God. I don't know what I thought would happen, but this was the beginning of our descent into almost Shakespearean madness and despair with The SS, and frustration, sadness, feelings of futility and so started the blame game. The problem is that you put off asking for help until you really really need it, and when they can't react it is devastating.

At a point when I was so frigging frustrated I wanted to shout so loud my head might pop off and bounce round the room like an effing pinball, I wrote to the Government Adoption Advisor, a lovely bloke called Martin Narey, himself adopted, a real advocate and a voice in a jumbled system. He had been extolling the virtues of a new "Adoption Support Fund". I'll give you an extract of the first letter I wrote, it's a bit serious, but might demonstrate just how helpless we felt...

"We thought we could cope.

And we have coped, for the past year... just.

Our adopted son's attachment issues were not evident at the beginning. Yes, he would have tantrums on a regular basis... yes, he does not care for any particular toy... yes, he has made no really close friends... and yes he has always had a pretty negative outlook on life, but he was ok in public, at school and with relatives, making amazing academic achievements ... and... we thought we could cope.

After the most dreadful school holiday we realised that his behaviour had deteriorated to such an extent that we needed help. His toys are discarded, his friendships superficial, his behaviour not always appropriate, his tantrums manifesting with others, his bond with us at most is shaky, his rejection of us evident. He needs help, that we can't give.

So I contacted the adoption team by email asking for support. A week and a half later he exhibited such inappropriate behaviour at school the Head suggested exclusion if it happened again. Our son's behaviour that day demonstrated to us and the School that he really has no concept of the right thing to do, and shows no remorse for his actions, only anger about being told off.

So the plea went in, please help, it is now urgent.

We have played email ping pong for 6 weeks now, whilst the post-adoption teams from each local authority try to decide who will fund anything, and who will undertake any new assessment. We have talked until blue about the issues, we are thinking of writing a pamphlet to describe the situation so we don't have to explain it again... the School are doing their best, they have put in place a CAF, unfortunately because there is a "waiting list" for post-adoption support (LA words not mine), no-one from post-adoption has attended any meeting, no worker has been allocated, no communication forthcoming, and we have a little boy who has had no intervention whatsoever. I have taken him to the GP, we are referred to a paediatrician, and surprise surprise we are on a waiting list.

In the last month amongst other things, he has screamed and screamed and screamed some more (probably 2 days a week he doesn't), until he feels sick, has hurt his tummy, and has lost his voice. He has disrupted his class to such an extent that most days he is sent out to calm down. His learning, has suffered. He has eaten 5 pairs of pyjamas, some marbles and started on his own fingers. His 6 year old sister has taken to wearing earmuffs inside to drown out the noise. This can't be right, can it? He's only 7, and he's hurting.

My husband and I have run out of ideas, the toolbox is empty, we did all the courses, we've read the books, we cannot get through to this little boy, his world revolves around him, and it is not a good world. We are sick of explaining to people over and over again, we are sick of dealing with the screaming, and the moods, we don't deserve this and neither does he. This is not a happy house, and this is a boy's life we are talking about.

So I'm glad that over 2000 people are benefitting from the ASF, I hope that they find the support that they and their children need. Your advocacy for adoptive families has really impressed me. These are people who may have had to jump huge hurdles to get where they are today, and it is good to see there are people out there who may understand what they go through. However I am not surprised that adoptions fail.

None of us want to be a statistic, but as I sit here waiting for a call from the adoption "support" team, to let me know the situation today, after having had no contact from them for 2 weeks, dreading going to pick him up from school, I am now acutely aware of how we can all become a number."

I re-wrote some time later in an email entitled "When no-one will listen"…

"I see that you will be stepping down from your position as Chair of the Adoption Leadership Board next year. I wanted to write while you still are in that position.

I attach a letter that I sent to an email address I found for you on your website, I guess that address was no longer correct so I'm trying again.

I wrote this on the 20th October, ***6 weeks after I asked for support, and 6 weeks ago****. So 3*

months after *my plea for help nothing has changed, we are in limbo, our son has had no support, and becomes more alien to us every day, the request for reassessment of needs by the children's adoption authority, has resulted in a local Social worker being allocated, she has not yet met the children.*

The bureaucracy of the local authority and funding arrangements for these children is a shambles. A little boy who at 7 is displaying signs that he is deeply troubled cannot access help without a fight. How can it take over 3 months to access anything? It's all about money, social services are too stretched, the placing authority have got two children off their hands and adopted, now there's a success, they don't have to spend any more time or money on them. My husband is seriously considering writing to our local MP to highlight a serious issue.

What about the adoptive parents? It's nearly Christmas, and we are exhausted. And that 7 year old boy? Well, no miracle has happened, his past hasn't gone away.

I hope this gets to you. All I want to do is vent my frustration at someone who may listen.

Many thanks"

... and he responded horrified he had not had my original email. We blooming rely on this modern technology, and it fails us, without us knowing. I am a self-confessed Luddite, but I still rely on this method of communication. Anyway somehow this message had found its wiggly way to him. He got on the case for us. We felt important to somebody. And we were for ten minutes. Sadly he quit the job, I don't blame him, but he empathised very well at the time.

"This is just to say I've received this (my adoption adviser email address has been unused for sometime and you should have got an out of office reply telling you that).

Even after all this time being involved in adopters' struggles I'm shocked to read this. I have no powers of investigation but I shall do what I can to help.

Can you send me a list of key dates, when the children were placed and so on and details of the placing LA and names of who you have been dealing with.

I'm so sorry you have been treated so poorly.

Kind Regards
Martin Narey

Martin Narey
Sir Martin Narey
Twitter: @martinnarey"

So I did as he asked and put together the sorry story on paper, well electronic paper, and sent it off. I suppose he may have rattled a few cages, as in the end someone did write to us, but by then Martin Narey had gone, and it was all just words… not even on real paper… That was five years ago.

Five years later we are rebuilding our lives. It feels looking back, like there was a moment we realised we were on the worst rollercoaster ever, where every time you think it's stopping it starts again. And you want to be sick, but you can't because someone else will end up seeing your breakfast the second time around. And you are sharing that rollercoaster with people you really wish you weren't, because they are the fun police. And those people see your face when you can't help screaming, and they can't cope either, because they also want to get off. And it's all very humiliating. Looking back I can hardly make sense of how we coped. When someone you love is going through something terrible you are desperate to help, but we felt helpless, and incapable.

It's All Just Balls

So, after repeatedly saying we were in crisis mode for months (certainly longer than a flipping Summer school holiday), the School getting on the case, the emails floating round the ether, we got another social worker. Yay! From a different team. Yay! Clearly an experienced lady, not a rusher, not emotional, not warm … full of fabulous ideas though. Have you tried x,y or z? Yes we bloody have. Do we look stupid? She actually came to visit after a month or so, and about a month after that, she sent round a theraplay expert. I should say Theraplay® (that's registered trademark you know), as it is a recognised way of helping families and children to build attachments through kind of playful and non-threatening but quite specific interactions. There's a lot of touching, sensory interaction and it's about building trust. I know this because we had swallowed a library worth of information about this stuff. It's actually a brilliant method, and has been used for probably fifty years with great success. I did believe in it. The problem was, here we go, another problem… we had been very clear, we were in crisis like six months before that, and we had told them everything we had tried, on our own, including this kind of thing.

The therapist, (sorry not therapist, social worker) was really nice, but she wasn't offering to be there and help us do this thing. My understanding was that they were meant to do some kind of assessment with the parent and child and then lead the play sessions accordingly. I don't mean to be rude, but when the very nice lady left me after an hour, I felt very awkward, with a bundle of cards about how to do it on my own, and with a load of cotton wool balls. I was asked if I had found it helpful, and being quite frank as is my wont, I said not really. We needed to go back further in developing any attachments. Things were broken. And nobody had actually seen Boy yet. We never saw Cotton Wool Social Worker again. Sadly this came to be portrayed as the first time I was reluctant to engage with the system. All because I didn't think that cotton wall balls were the answer to the problem at that stage. Believe me, if I could use cotton wool balls to solve things, I bloody would. I love those little fluffy nuggets. So at the start there was no help, when we asked, there was no help when we really needed it. And when we got someone who could get us help, there was no help. By the time Cotton Wool lady came round I hope you can understand why I was rather taken aback by the pathetic suggestion that they thought would make a difference at a time of crisis. Trying to make the problem fit the solution. Not listening. Ticky boxes. And so yet again it appeared it was all down to us to do it.

We had found out that about six months before, there was this fund put in place for people like us to pay for targeted support, and the good news was that whatever was needed could be provided. £19 million (pardy?! How much?!) of government funding on top of what was already available. Indulge me in a quote from their own information. This fund would pay for "an in-depth assessment of the child and family's needs with a focus on trauma and attachment, and how this demonstrates the links to the assessment of support needs. Led and undertaken by a qualified clinician. Result in a therapeutic support plan for the child(ren) / family." This sounds amazing doesn't it? It is how I came across the Government Adoption Advisor, as he was a big advocate of this, and rightly so. Finally, they were putting in place proper funding for people as I said, like us.

Obviously we didn't need £19 million, but a few quid should help. Now that was hope-giving. We just needed to work out what was needed. Our view?

Something direct, someone to see him and assess him in some way, an expert. Not like Cotton Wool lady, who told us to tickle his feet, and left us to it, surrounded by discarded little balls of fluff. Whoever invented this Adoption Support Fund had the right idea. You just needed an assessment of needs to be done, by your local authority, who will decide whether therapeutic support is needed. Well as I said I had already taken him to the GP, who was definitely maybe, going to refer us, but I looked forward to meeting someone expert in this area. In fact as it turns out this new social worker was to do the assessment. I am not sure how she had qualified in any arena that would have enabled her to decide whether therapeutic support was necessary, in light of the Adoption Support Fund's own statement as quoted, but at the time I didn't think about that, this was means to an end. As I said, she was not a rusher. In fact it was like she was bored, of people, of life.

So, six sodding months it took to do this assessment. Six months of sheer hell on earth. Looking at how we parent, basically looking to see what we might be doing wrong. At the same time because the school were fully engaged they started a process of meetings gathering together people who could help, called a

Common Assessment Framework (CAF). I lost track of how many times over that period I sat there incredulous, as so-called professionals and mostly Bored Social Worker if she turned up, sat there saying and contributing nothing, no progress was made, the school tried everything in their repertoire but between us we were all bimbling around clueless. And Boy was six months older, and we had six months more trauma and fighting. This is just to get a report written to apply for funding, not to receive the funding or get the support, six months to write a frigging report. Good grief, it's a good job she wasn't on piece work. During this period I think she really felt she got to know Boy, from meeting him, just twice.

We got the writing to people bug, we wanted to let people know what was going on, to galvanise some help. We wrote to somebody of importance at the original SS Headquarters, and copied our letter to our local MP. We weren't trying to cause trouble, but we had to do something. Here is one of our extracts, I like an extract…

"We are writing to you in sheer desperation and in the hope that by doing so, we

might mobilise the right support from your organisation...

...We adopted siblings from your County three years ago....

...We feel that since the adoption (the Local Authority) has completely abandoned us and because we are out of County, there has been little engagement, erratic communication with no continuity and that the child, is not being placed at the centre by Social Services. Quite honestly, it feels that (The Local Authority) has abrogated all responsibility and that the hoops of Adoption Panel etc that we went through to adopt, where the mantra that 'the best interests of the child are always at the centre' has proven both hollow and hypocritical in practice, beyond placement. We have tried to access assistance through the School, NHS and Fredshire Social Service to get a CAHMS referral and put in place clinical diagnosis and then support for a very damaged, challenged and struggling little boy, who is the funding responsibility of Bobshire for some time yet, but we have failed to get him the funding for the support framework he so desperately needs.

There are many champions of (Boy), the school in particular, but sadly they do not have the resources, professional medical status or power to do much other than try to support him and us as his parents. We have not yet managed to motivate bureaucracy to access adoption support funding or get him assessed and clinically diagnosed with reactive attachment disorder or whatever it is he is suffering from and put in place the necessary action to support (Boy). We could probably turn this around if (Boy) could access the help he so desperately needs – but we as parents have no more tools to deal with this and no one seems keen on giving us any. The longer it goes on, the more damage is done. Quite frankly it is a travesty and a tragedy. We, as parents, wake up every day with a sense of foreboding and feel that we are failing (Boy), failing his sister and failing ourselves...

...So the foot dragging, lame bureaucracy, the absence of responsibility or a child centric approach are contributing to what feels like an almost unavoidable catastrophe, when all it would take is some effort, contact, care, recognition, engagement and resources. We took on these two

children willingly and will champion their cause because they are ours, we will fight for (Boy) whilst ever we see it as in his and our best interest as a family. Please don't send people to talk to us unless they are constructive and empowered to swiftly bring resources to bear – we have talked enough about it. We do not want platitudes, we need action"

Crikey, rereading that now, it sounds a bit cross, doesn't it, and a bit threatening. Can't really believe we sent that around. Then again, it does show how we were trying to use our frustrations to actually get somewhere, rather than sitting wringing our hands.

We got a response to this at least, it was full of this kind of thing…

"Your letter has brought into focus the difficulties faced by adoptive families when children are placed outside of Bobshire County Council. We are currently undergoing a review of procedures that will ensure families like yours and that formal agreements with placing authorities

are entered into so that families will not be left bereft of support when they need it".

Which was interesting, not that we thought it would get us anywhere. Was this them actually admitting that there was a problem with procedures, and the lack of support given to adoptive families? Not really, it was rather a limp biscuit of a letter.

We then received a visit from The SS from that first county after the letter. A sandal wearing, satchel carrying sort of social worker, (He was a he by the way, the first we had met, not that it matters, as it made no difference). He promised to try to help. With him he accidentally brought a copy of the above letter from their Head of Children's Services. Well it wasn't actually a copy, it was a previous version which rather admitted responsibility where the new version which we officially received admitted nothing of the sort, and blamed our local authority. I still have these letters, although I am not sure what to do with them!

The undelivered letter also said

"the adoption support fund criteria also changed during this time with the Local Authority within which the adopter lives now enabled to make applications to the fund but that permission in writing is needed. This delayed your support and for that I apologise as it appears ***the child was not kept at the centre of our intervention****".*

It's the whole point. Keeping the child at the centre of everything. Sadly this admission didn't help at all. Partly because we shouldn't have been given that version of the letter, they obviously rethought what they were saying. And so what? We must all move forward no blame, nobody at fault. The good news is that The SS have already learned the lessons we have identified we should have learnt, so that is great, box ticked.

Satchel Social Worker sat and listened and made some notes, which he put in his satchel at the end and scurried off back to Bobshire, tripping over his sandals in his haste to depart. Never to be heard of again. Quite literally their representative represented them for an hour and then buggered off into the sunset. We seem to have that effect on people on a regular basis.

We did then get a psychologist. Bored Social Worker brought the authority one with her at an early meeting. I am afraid I didn't really get on with her. All right, all right, don't roll your eyes. It's just that she offended me. This had not happened regularly in my life, but all of a sudden I found I was being told by someone who I found rather domineering that I had just met, that I was literally doing it all wrong. Again without seeing the subject of her pronouncements, no meeting Boy. I bristled, they left and I told husband there was no way I could work with this lady. She herself had actually come across as quite mad, and I almost wanted to give her a psychological assessment. Bored Social Worker had sat and nodded her way through this occasion, lapping it up and interjecting with her own opinions and they had a lovely mutual appreciation society meeting in front of me. When they decided that we actually could do with someone to help, they sent this Apparently Mad Psychologist on her own, and then another one so we could compare and yes I am going to be rude, where we felt the original one could do with her own help, the other one was young and fragrant, and quite human, so we picked her, Young Psycholady. This was six months after the idea was first mooted. six months seems to be the target. That's half a year if I do my sums right. That's a long bollocky time in a child's life isn't it? And the months kept just passing with so little progress.

Someone's Pooping Marbles

Boy was observed at school, they found him to be behaving rather oddly. He would get up from his desk, if he had managed to sit down, wander around the class, making strange noises, disturb the other children, demand and then reject attention, chewed his pencils so much they were dangerous, refuse to work, fidget, fiddle. On the question of chewing things, did I mention he ate his bed? Not all of it obviously, but I began to notice shards of wood on the floor, and realised that like a little beaver he had chewed a huge groove in the red wood, some splinters falling off, the rest he must have swallowed! He chewed the buttons on his duvet, the pillowcase, gulped down marbles, lego, nibbled his way through school jumpers, pens, and goodness knows what else. Sorry but did you know marbles don't flush away. I had noticed something in our loo and on closer inspection realised that this was not one of your normal deposits. How could it have got there I asked myself? I thought I must be going mad and then I realised, Duh. Stoopid. Luckily what goes in generally comes out and the inspections of the toilet bowl were made on occasions with incredulity.

We realised in fact that everything he owned had bite marks in it somewhere. We brought it to the attention of Bored Social Worker, who of course thought he was hugely anxious during the night and that explained it all didn't it. He was moved around the class on a regular basis, normally after he had sat next to a massively sensible child to help him, and then would say he was going to kill them, which caused a little upset. Can't imagine why. He was sent out of class, kept in class, given blue tac to fiddle with to help him concentrate, he made intricate models with it instead of working, then ate them, given pencil toppers to chew on, which he ate. We gave him indestructible chew toys, which he managed to consume with some gusto in just one night.

We knew that he needed success, and something like homework, riding a bike, learning to read, although traumatic for all of us, when he could do it, gave him a glow, and a sense of achievement. But the struggle to get him to that point wore us down, every time. He wanted to do everything, he wanted to have everything. As soon as he did it, he was the world's expert and didn't need to do it again, and as soon as he got something, he discarded it, looking for the next thing. He went from achieving above average for his age to dropping behind. We were shocked, as whilst we only wanted him to achieve his potential, he had proved himself extremely intelligent and bright and such a quick learner, and to drop behind was such a shame for him.

The SS expert, Bored Social Worker, told us it was basically what they call "attachment difficulties". We just needed to alter how we parented and eventually it would change. We agreed Boy definitely had these attachment issues. We said that at the start you plonkers. He had no real bond with anyone or anything, and was still indiscriminate if he ever showed affection. We really believed we might benefit from expert CAMHS assessment and support. We were convinced that there were underlying issues with him that might be identified and provide a base from which to go forwards. You know I had taken him to the GP to get a referral. The GP did refer us to the county paediatrician or whatever his title was… who referred it straight back, couldn't help, he was adopted, it was attachment which was **not a mental health problem.** We were not happy. No-one would see him. So we pushed it, and eventually they deigned to allow me to a discussion meeting with CAMHS, I thought to myself that finally I was getting somewhere. What a set up, an ambush. Apparently Mad Psychologist, who we had rejected was there. The Bored Social Worker, and two others also sat there like a jury. They made me present the case for him to be seen by CAMHS, there and then with no warning. They had lots of information which I didn't have, all his background, which we had never got. It seemed there had been discussions over the information from that assessment we were waiting for, by the expert in these matters, Bored Social Worker. At this point we had not seen the assessment she had started all those months before, so that was a little unfair I thought. They sent me away with a flea in my ear. They said unfortunately that as it was clear his issues were down to attachment, they would not see him ever, the reason being that … wait for it … this was **not a "mental health issue",** it was all attachment. On the way out the door Bored Social Worker presented me with the Assessment she had done, which we had been desperate for, I can't imagine why she couldn't get it to me before the CAMHS meeting that day, unless she really really didn't want to, she skipped off, and I went home with even more trepidation, holding this piece of work.

Interestingly I read an article by Sally Donovan (Adoption Support – the tanker is turning. https://www.sallydonovan.co.uk/2017/09/29/adoption-support-tanker-turning/) over a year later, where she talks about CAMHS appearing "to be mostly absent, because it rolled its eyes when 'trauma', 'attachment' and 'early adversity' were mentioned, because it was able to declare 'these are **not mental health issues'** and 'we do not treat adopted or fostered children' (yes really) and because of its propensity to 'medicalise' and medicate symptoms and send parents on inappropriate parenting courses. It was and is also chronically lacking in funding. All this left an enormous, howling void of distress.". How is it possible that CAMHS had said almost word for word the same thing to me a year and a half earlier. Do they have a script? It wouldn't have been so bad if they had on their script some suggestions as to who might help. But they didn't. Welcome back to limbo land.

Hub was horrified at the treatment I had got at CAMHS so pushed for another meeting. This time Young Psycholady went with him. I had more hope, he was fired up and that was normally productive. When he got back that day he was in bits. He had got very upset, he was completely fobbed off, they told him they were not going to do anything, they had already told me that so couldn't understand why he was there. Dead end. They got their script out again and told him, guess what, that because

Boy was adopted, all this was due to attachment problems, not a mental health issue so eff off. No alternative suggestions, just eff off. So off he effed.

So we finally had the draft assessment. Actually I think Bored Social Worker felt that her assessment was finished when she sent it to us for our comment. Ha, how little she really knew us. Asking us to comment on a document that commented about us was like asking Dog to comment on your harmonica playing. She would howl for hours. We couldn't just comment, it was blatantly wrong in parts, badly written and opinionated. To be honest we read it with horror, as it yet again put the blame at our door. There were plenty of opinions in it, about Boy, and us. What manner of crap was this? A blame fest was what it was, not helpful, not balanced, objective, or professional. Well, that's my humble opinion.

This monstrosity was scattered throughout with comments about the fact that I would not engage, I hadn't tried or wouldn't try group therapy, that during some visits Hub was not present. For feck's sake, he had a high-pressured job, which provided the roof over our head. She pronounced that "The parents are stuck in a despondent cycle that makes it difficult to respond to suggestions and strategies." I could swear. Who was she to say this? Yes, we were effing despondent, partly due to the lack of support, but it certainly did not mean that weren't trying every single day and that we wouldn't try something, anything, if we hadn't already and if we thought there was any way it would help. We spent a long time deliberating over which battles to fight, and eventually sent in some amendments (factual) to be incorporated. We were very clear on our views about her document, which at the end of the day would go in Boy's records, and he may one day read them. Rather than incorporate them she sort of tagged them onto the end as additions in red ink, and it was made very clear that these were our opinions, not hers. Our tagged on response (Her comments underlined, then ours) was along the lines of:

(Parents) have FAILED to:

- *Use the blanket and nurturing – we now use this every time – but the situation when he has a tantrum is not a nurturing one and is usually the result of a direct challenge.*
- *Use Theraplay – will people please listen to us and stop judging us – they might then understand us and actually help us.*

- *<u>Join any groups</u> – not ruled out – just a very generic approach as it has been offered so far*
- *<u>Training</u> – Practical parenting – we are open and willing to discuss how this might help – again we are unsure how targeted*
- *<u>Placement Services Therapist</u> – absolutely – but we need to find the right relationship.*
- *<u>Parents anger is preventing them from accessing The LA's</u> resources – Parents are trying to channel all of their energy positively for (Boy) – to get him the support he so desperately needs – to hold our family together. We do not feel hugely well supported in that. We feel quite critically judged in this draft report.*
- *<u>Boy's utter rejection of Mum is partly fuelled by Mum's response to him.</u> This is an opinion – Parents hold an entirely different one.*

As you can see, her comments were pretty damning.

We asked for some actions. She tagged this on the end too:

What action are Parents asking for:

- *Professional Diagnosis*
- *Targeted (3rd party) interventions to help (Boy) understand himself*
- *Targeted (3rd party) interventions to help Parents support (Boy), (Girl) and each other.*
- *A multi agency coordinated and fully resourced approach to support (Boy).*

Why

- *So he understands his place in the world and is more comfortable in his own skin*
- *So he can function really well in society*
- *So he is happy and can thrive*

We felt awful, all these things that we had written, rather clumsily unincorporated, clearly her beliefs in no way aligning with ours. In fact the way she did it kind of made us look like complete idiots who just wouldn't listen, and refused to do anything basically. If parents who are desperately seeking support are placed in an adversarial place, they will fight. That's why they are parents isn't it? To fight for their children? We showed people who we trusted, what she had written and they couldn't believe it. But we were also embarrassed, this was proper criticism, and it involved a child's life. The fact she made a point of marking out that these were our views instead of discussing it with us demonstrated how far our relationship had come. Nevertheless we let it go, as we needed to get funding for something. We naively assumed that there would be somebody who would look and say, this boy needs to see this person. But talk about damp squib. The assessment was submitted and we waited to see what was next.

Suck It Up Buttercup

The more you are treated in a particular way, the more you start to question yourself, and I reckon around this time we probably started to do this. On the one hand it seemed bleeding obvious. If a child had an issue, which had been identified, then that child would need help with it, be it physical or mental, and those around should help to support that child. On the other hand we were constantly being told that the issues he was presenting with were actually our problem. We couldn't change him, we needed to change ourselves. But we were not arguing that we couldn't help, change the way we parented him, but we did argue that somebody really ought to meet him first, and try to really target support to him and us. We argued that we were in shock, at the changes in him that were taking place. We argued that we had been thrown into a situation which we were completely unprepared for, and although the weekly meetings with Young Psycho lady were helpful in that there was a third party who could help us to talk things through between us, this wasn't actually looking at the bigger picture, and she never actually met him. A child who was desperately unhappy and struggling to function in his world. She was helping us survive, nothing else.

I'm not saying that there was an agenda from the start, but all the talk was totally aimed at getting us to do things differently. It was bizarre, because still no-one saw him but us. Oh, and School. School were in the same boat. They saw the boy they thought they knew transform into a totally different being. Now excuse me, but we may have been new parents, but they were not a new school, not new teachers. Where we only had instinct, they had seen most things. They didn't know what to do either. No-one was going in there and telling them it was their fault. Basically we were argumentative weren't we? And the longer it went on the more we were made to feel shit. The more we were told we were doing it wrong, the more we floundered. It was self-fulfilling.

We managed to get some sessions with a place where traumatised children went for therapy. The School had suggested it, the brilliant School. The SS agreed, but the massive funding of £50 a week couldn't be sorted by them. So the school were so angry for us, they paid. I took a personal cheque in to cover the cost, we were so embarrassed. This was totally unacceptable, this was our problem not the school's. They assured me not to worry, they would get the money back, they just wanted to do something. They also fought to get him an Education and Health Care Plan (EHCP), formerly known as a statement. With no diagnosis, no expert help, no guidance, new issues, they got him a serious plan, which stated he needed funding for 30 hours of help. Which they used wisely, not throwing people at him, but support, and thought. And which was amazing and testament to the commitment of the school to the children in their care. So now he had one hour a week with an art therapist, who was really lovely, but with no prior suggestions as to what he needed she started from scratch with him. At the same time I had to attend parenting skills sessions, which basically traumatised me. I'm not one for talking about feelings, and these did take place in a reception area, with other parents who ranged from quite happy people whose children had a recognised issue, to people who were about to be evicted from their flat, and have their benefits stopped for whatever reason, and whose children were at risk in some way. Talk about how down to earth with a bump. I could not hide.

The main suggestion of Mrs Miggins, the very earnest group leader, was self-help. You need to go to a spa, find some time, sort out your own parachute before you sort your child's!! Thanks for that. I didn't think of that. I told them that I couldn't do it any more. They then wanted me in the sessions with Boy, but he seemed so uncomfortable, that I couldn't do that. I tried, and as soon as he realised I was going to be there he acted up, which completely compromised the trusting relationship that the therapist was trying to build. And the session became stressful for him. So I was then told to go back to the sessions with Mrs Miggins. But at least his sessions were something directly for him.

We were still seeing Young Psycho lady, to try to work out our thoughts and feelings, sort of supervision. She would stay for two or three hours looking at how we had done things with Boy. It gave us vital space to process, together, as we had got to a point where we couldn't talk about the situation, as it just upset us. So that was two mornings a week, an additional morning every six weeks in a meeting at School, meetings with Bored Social Worker, meetings with school, living with his behaviour, and trying to work a bit in between. Girl had so little of our time, and was rarely the focus of attention, in thoughts or actions. I resented this for her I suppose. But she was fine, wasn't she? We have no idea how that period really affected her. She was as bright and breezy and glass half full as ever. A little challenging, but she got on with life in spite of it all. A bit like Dog who met every visitor with a lick, and a few more licks if they were canine averse. In fact then she would plonk herself on their feet, in a doggy attempt to ingratiate herself. She cracked on, when Boy was not there she was, when he was, she was to be found secreted in a quiet place, all forlorn, with only a plant pot for company.

Holidays And All that

At some point we decided we needed a break. We had asked about the possibility of respite for a weekend now and then, something which is common for foster carers. If only they could identify a suitably trained person Boy could go to for us all to have a break from the intensity of it all. It took an age but eventually The SS decided they probably could do this, and would put out a search for a respite carer. But we would have to tread very carefully and prepare Boy and have a meeting with the carer and not let him think we were sending him away. Jesus. They really thought we were a pair of prats. Anyhoo, after a couple of months Bored Social Worker emailed us just as she went on leave, to say that they had identified a respite carer for a weekend. A number of issues with this sprung to us, bearing in mind the sage advice over all the prep we should do with him. The date she was proposing was next effing weekend, so there could be no preparation time and oh, did I forget to say, the CAMHS guy had in the meantime said that under no circumstances would he recommend that Boy went for respite without his sister, as this would add massively to his attachment problems. We couldn't believe it. Left hand right hand? Arse or elbow?

What the hell were we supposed to do then? Facing another two week school holiday with the strain of dealing with it on our own. Don't ever dare to have a problem needing The SS at a weekend or during a holiday. Our wonderful parents though concocted a plan where if Boy wanted he could stay with them one after the other and we could stay with Girl if she wanted. This gave us a dilemma. We knew that he would enjoy himself, with all that attention and no real demands, we knew that she would relish the idea too. We knew that this had taken a lot for our families to offer as caring for him was so draining. But we had to do something. So we decided that it wasn't exactly doing what CAMHS guy had said not to do, as it was family, so we gave the children the choice separately. Come skiing or go to Grannies? And we would live with the decision. I couldn't quite believe the response. Boy said he would rather not come skiing. Girl was desperate to come. So that was that. It sounds utterly odd I know, but he was at this point constantly expressing his views about us, and how he didn't want to be with us. Maybe we should have not done it, maybe we should have forced him to come, or not gone, and had an intense period of reinforcing the family unit. But we didn't. When he was so convincing, and insistent, we took our parents up on their offer.

So when the ridiculously late response (to us having said we would not pursue the respite) came back from Social Services, along with the comment "I hope you are having a lovely Easter holiday…" we told them that they were clearly not in the loop, that the CAMHS specialist, who offered no help, had said not to do respite and we had made our own arrangements. So in that week Boy exhausted the patience and kindness of our parents, worried them greatly, raised so many questions in them about his demeanour, attitude, mental health. They didn't put demands on him, they pandered to him. He threw it back at them, he ran away, he was wildly inappropriate with other people. They were absolutely exhausted by the end of the week, although they didn't admit that until a lot later. We had a weirdly good time. So did Girl. Does this sound peculiar? It was. We felt pangs of guilt, relief, happiness, remorse, every emotion. Looking back I can't criticise us for doing it. He didn't want to be with us, and we allowed him not to be.

The second time we were given a chance for a break came a little while later. Grandparents again. They were trying to stop us falling apart and felt they had to do something. So they said they would have both children, and we should get away for a long weekend. I was so excited. This time no guilt. BOTH children were going to Grannies and so that was OK. Then Monsieur L'Appendicitis paid a visit. For four days we stayed by Boy's bed whilst he recovered from a perforated appendix. Whilst he was slightly sedated he was calm and responded well to us. We thought this must have been such a shock to him. Subconsciously these people are caring for me and there for me, and maybe I don't need to reject them. We were hopeful in adversity, sensed a possibility of a change in relationships.

We knew he was feeling better though when he started. He ignored us, refused to speak to us, and literally when the nurse came to tell him he could come home he suddenly was in great pain again, even though five minutes earlier he was leaping about the bed as we tried to get him to be calm. They saw through him and sent him home. It was bizarre. It made it worse not better. I drove for eight hours to take Girl up to grandparents, she needed a break, and then home to care for Boy, who just wouldn't respond to anything we did or said. Including the need to chill. He had our full attention, no Girl to share us with, but he just wanted to be somewhere else. One day he went outside. I found him on the trampoline, that well know calming down device. Result, he bust his stitches, and I had to shuffle back with him to the nurse, to show what a bad parent I was yet again. He loved the attention though.

I don't know what possessed me but I guess it was an attempt to show myself how strong I was, and I decided to take the children to France for the first week of a two week holiday in the Summer. On my own. Hub was massively busy, and I thought it would show how supportive I was giving him some time to himself. He was to join us after a week. On the drive when we were leaving I cried internally, and did that gulp thing to swallow it. I couldn't see for about the first mile of the journey, until I gave myself a virtual slap round the face and told myself that I was a grown up and how lucky I was to be going on holiday and that we might achieve that lemonade lifestyle in the middle of nowhere with no stresses, just us and the sun, and lots of food, and the great outdoors with only the moo moos in the field next door for company. We drove over, took about ten hours. I have blanked out the week, my memory is hazy, but looking at photographs, it was definitely sunny we did the stuff we should have done, ate sausages in pancakes and ice cream, went to the beach, played games.

I made sure they were in separate rooms, and we stuck to routines, because Boy fought sleep so much, and would wake up so early and start prodding and poking Girl and then hell would break loose. But I did it, I was brave. Hub arrived and whether it was a build up of emotion or excitement, the moment he walked through the door, there was a hoohah from Boy over something, which rumbled on and off for the next seven days, and I think Hub spent most of that time wishing he hadn't bothered. It was awful. We argued about it, I just wanted to walk out, in fact I did one evening, down the road, thinking I would not go back. I did of course, I didn't have my passport, so I might have been an illegal immigrant. I find it hard thinking back, about what went through my head that day. I was at the end of a very long tether, with another couple of tethers attached. What didn't help was that in leaping off my seat instinctively to stop Boy stabbing his sister with a knife over their dinner one day, my back went so that putting one foot in from of another was insane agony. The first time I had ever had back pain, adding to the list of woe is me's.

I drove the children home via the ferry at the end, where they were both sick. My car got a flat tyre, my windscreen wipers got stuck on for the entire journey, which was one of those beautiful sunny Summer days. The French mechanic I popped to see on the way said he could turn them off but then if it rained I was in trouble, so we left them on, and by the time we got home the squeak of rubber on dry window was like some kind of medieval torture device. Marvellous, just to top everything off, boy was so rude to someone during the crossing that my jaw hit the floor.

All we were trying to do was have a good life, and it was like someone was looking down on me seeing how much I would take before spontaneous combustion. I haven't explained how stressful it was to have them in the car together. Downright dangerous probably. He once tried to open the car door as Granddad was driving along at 50 miles an hour. Boy undid his seatbelt, he again prodded and poked Girl, I cannot tell you, they never slept. So after about ten hours on the road that day, I stopped to pump up my tyre again, and to get a break from the whinging windscreen wipers, and the thought even crossed my mind to get him out of the car and leave him behind. Which again of course I didn't. I made it back. And swore I would never do it again.

One Step Forward, Two Steps Back

So we were now reliant on The SS. Young Psycholady decided that the situation might benefit from some external thoughts. She had an idea about eventually getting us to a point where we could use some DDT, or DDP. Not the insecticide, banned in many countries, although apparently it was used to control malaria, yellow fever, typhus, lice, and bubonic plague, with a list like that maybe we should have tried it, we might have tried anything! No, this one was Dyadic Developmental Therapy, a whole family approach, but also meaning that Boy could be actually seen by someone, we were rather persistent in our view that this might actually shed some light on any underlying issues. She started to do a bit of a search around for external agencies who we might benefit from seeing. This was good. Funnily enough there was no one in the local area, I was starting to wonder about our local area. We were not in some godforsaken backwater, but what the hell happens in bigger towns, people must get completely misplaced in the system. But she found, goodness knows how, an organisation 100s of miles away who she said might help.

We were a little disappointed that the people who came to assess him (or us) although coming from a well-respected organisation, were all about attachment disorders, they were attachment professionals, and we did make no bones about it to them that they were not what we had hoped for. We knew there were those issues, although we were looking for help to deal with them, we wanted to see if there was anything else going on. But, nearly a year after our first visit from Bored Social Worker, someone was coming to meet Boy and that was better than nothing. So two days were set aside for their visit at the end of the Summer holiday. The first day was spent basically interviewing us, on tape and on camera, looking at our views, our parenting styles, how we were parented, our attachment styles, yes, us again. A thorough going over, everything laid bare. Next day, both children, were observed, tested, videoed. … played the game. He was polite, and his speech precise and strangely clipped, and he did everything as we had expected, said what he thought they wanted to hear, survival instinct in full flow. They said they could see through it. And I think they did. The moment they went through the front gate he imploded, then exploded, and was then back to his normal self. We were wrung out.

When the report came through we read it and our fears were realised. It was mostly about how we were able to parent. But at least the recommendations were therapy, that any further move would be catastrophic for Boy, but then they also suggested unusually, that Boarding School might be an option later on, to enable him to remain within a family, but for us all to have periods of separation in order to be able to strengthen ourselves again. Completely the opposite of the CAMHS warning. His problem was the mother figure. He couldn't cope with it, and had utterly rejected any attempt from me to become that person. I knew that, thanks. But now someone else was saying it, and in fact they didn't blame me. They were actually quite complementary about us for a change.

This boarding school thing became quite a topic of debate. We had not thought of it, except in the sense that quite a few of our friends children had gone to private schools, where some boarded, and turned out rather well. Whilst we always hoped that this time next year we would be millionaires, that kind of schooling for our children was a pipe dream. But someone was suggesting that this might be a good option for Boy. There were grants available too.

Was this the long-term solution? Would that take the pressure off everybody, and at the same time give him opportunities that we could never give him. We didn't know but it was an interesting thought, worthy of further discussion.

We needed to do something with this report and a meeting was suggested to discuss it. Unfortunately the Local Authority would have to pay for this, who knew that meetings with leading private practitioners were not free?! Well yes, it doesn't take the brains of an archbishop. It took a couple of months to sort this shocking revelation out. We also discovered that this £5000 (! I am so in the wrong job) assessment had been done at risk, as no confirmation of funding had been given to the providers by The SS. We were grateful to the organisation for doing this, but it served to add weight to our personal growing concerns about the priorities of The SS. When they had finally sorted out that they could in fact pay for this follow up meeting (half price negotiated!) because otherwise what was the point of the assessment in the first place, Hub went along with the people who had assessed Boy to meet the Bored Social Worker and her Head Honcho boss, she being a very important lady, also being the one who allocates social workers to families, and who seemed to be the one holding the purse strings.

We hoped they would be willing to discuss one of the new suggestions which was to support us in finding a school for Boy, eventually, where he could board. This was an off the wall thought, but we had really thought about this new concept and entertained the idea that it would allow us the space during the week to recoup our strength and also that as his attachment problems were mainly with me as the mother figure this difficulty would be overcome by the school becoming the figure of authority hopefully allowing us to parent from a distance. We started to wonder if this kind of arrangement was the only choice for keeping the family together and would give him so many opportunities without the pressure of every day family life. But we needed the support of the Local Authority due to us not having bottomless pockets, or an offshore bank account. We had found a charity who would help with the funding, and whose arguments were similar to the professionals who had suggested it, but without Authority support it was a non-starter. My husband tried to use the whole life cost argument, that if Boy was in care it would cost them a lot more, in so many ways, especially financially. Surely that would sway them. We felt like someone was advocating to the Authority on our behalf and that really helped and motivated us. At this stage any new ideas were welcomed and anyone seeming to take our views and represent us was like some kind of revelation.

Around this time we had come to a conclusion. We had decided that we could no longer work with Bored Social Worker. For whatever reason our relationship was not productive, and the thought of having to constantly try to engage her was starting to add stress to our situation. In our view she had failed to attend meetings, was unfriendly and opinionated. It felt like the system was failing us and she, poor woman, effectively represented that system, in fact she was the human (almost) manifestation of the failure. Her attitude when she deigned to attend meetings, with others, her utter lack of empathy or understanding, had contributed in us arriving at a dark place and so we politely requested that maybe we might be able to work with someone else. We felt rather guilty, she probably thought she was doing everything she could, she was so thick-skinned. It didn't help that during one of her visits to us we had so much to say that she decided to run away. Hub quite frankly chased her down the garden path. She couldn't get away quick enough. That, and the obnoxious comments in the assessment, were probably the beginning of the end. I just don't think she could deal with us. We were obviously so difficult.

A couple of months after saying we were "incompatible" they had employed another lady on a year's contract, and she was allocated us to put up with. Bored Social Worker brought this one to meet us, and she was fine. They were like a double act, but not a comedy one. Of course this new social worker was "fine", they are all fine at the start. You think it doesn't matter whether you like them or not, you can be neutral about that, we didn't set out not to get on with people, all we were doing was fighting for our Boy. This one had a similar background to us, she had a bit of a twitch when she was nervous, and I think we must have made her nervous, because she did seem to twitch a lot. I'm not surprised though, since we had rejected her colleague, she probably had all sorts of preconceived ideas about us. Anyway we tried to engage with her. As it turns out, over time she seemed to become more and more opinionated than the previous one. She would spout that pop psychology at us, about how Boy's behaviour was due to one thing or another. I don't remember her showing me her psychology certificate. All we needed her to do was to facilitate us finally getting access to support for Boy, but she grated on us. We took time off to see her to chat about stuff, each time thinking we would get further forward. We didn't want to chat to her. This wasn't about having a lovely afternoon tea. This was serious.

I can't remember if she ever met the children. Maybe she didn't. She normally arranged a meeting in school hours. Actually take that back, I do recall she did meet Boy once. She arranged a meeting at school, with him. To ascertain his "views and wishes". When she had taken over our case she had instantly changed Boy's status to that of a "Child in Need", and it was something to do with that. I thought that it was a bit like being under suspicion to see your eight year old child without you present, when the person talking to him is not a trained psychologist, to ask your child about what they wanted, so I requested that someone from school was present at the meeting, or at least in the adjoining room. Partly because of the way in which he responded and had that interesting effect on adults who didn't know him, and depending on his mood all sorts of things could result. I didn't ask to be there myself, but surely an independent observer would be a good idea. I had no idea what she was going to ask him, but it made me very uncomfortable. She refused. She saw him on her own, goodness only knows what they talked about. We realised then, that she was the system reincarnated, it didn't matter what we wanted, and whether we were actually talking about our son, if she wanted to do something she was going to do it. The thing is you have to treat these people as means to an end, and so we felt that if we went in guns blazing we would totally put backs up, and get ourselves nowhere. We probably should have been more strident and not so polite, but every week that went past we thought this will be it, we'll get somewhere. We let her do her thing, we did not protest too much.

Our boy seemed to be regressing. He screamed and screamed like a toddler, and shouted, and crashed and bashed, and tested, and was destructive. You couldn't trust him with other children really. It was like he was un-developing. In the middle of one of his tantrums he kicked me in the face, and gave me a real shiner. When I got called into see the Headmaster (with my swollen eye) to talk about Boy stabbing a pencil in someone's face, I admitted I should have told School what had happened to me just in case. But these were all unrelated accidents, weren't they? Just him not seeing the consequences of his actions. Acting in the moment. In the same way as the unrelated incident when I lost two kitchen knives, subsequently found in his bedroom. Hub made sure that the School were told, as were The SS. School implemented some safety precautions, which is how they found the scissors, which he had secreted down his trousers on one of his 50 trips a day to the toilet. Oh and the ones he "lost" outside. The SS were very helpful. They said we should put sharp objects out of his reach! You what? Effing pathetic. You can stab someone with a blunt spoon if you try hard enough. I suppose at this point we started wondering to ourselves about how maturity would really affect him. As he got bigger how would these outbursts present. When he got to secondary school, or puberty hit, how would he express himself. What was going through his head?

People would say he's regressing and that is good. He is like a toddler, he can't explain what is wrong, he just feels like something is awry. We knew that at first. But then he was seven, he was eight, he was nine, he wasn't a baby and wouldn't let you treat him like one. What do we do? Wrap him in a blanket, soothe, empathise. Use the PACE method. What's this I hear you cry? Well, you try using Playfulness to help overcome this situation, and find some positive way forward, and you find yourself faced with a child who takes that playfulness as encouragement and completely explodes, uncontrollably. The last thing you feel is playful, you are tired, you have to suppress your own feelings and make this come naturally, fake it. Acceptance, of them, of their needs, feelings, thoughts. Fine, accepted. But what does this do? Encourages the behaviour. It's supposed to be about accepting the self, the inner child. Then the Curiosity. The phrase "I'm wondering…" has now become entrenched. But as he got older and we wondered out loud, he wondered why we wondered all the time, he got wise to it and would be ready for the wondering. Finally, be Empathetic. Try and get across that you understand how difficult things are for them, and combined with all the other PACE techniques, the child can hopefully learn that adults are unquestionably there for them, no strings attached and come to terms with their own feelings. But maybe we weren't cut out for it, maybe we did it wrong, maybe we just ran out of energy, we didn't understand, we couldn't empathise, we struggled, every single day and night, and he got worse and worse.

I noticed sometimes that as I tried to engage Boy, a weird thing would happen to his eyes. It looked like they went completely black and then there was nothing there, no feeling. This was so strange that I asked Mr Google. My friend Google came up with some research by an organisation called Attachment Disorder Maryland, (www.attachmentdisordermaryland.com/parenting.htm), which said:

1) Clear / bright- indicates that the child is present, engaged, in a positively balanced mood and more aware of the big picture.

2) Dark- the eyes appear as if a shadow has fallen across them and this usually reflects anger, rage, or depression.

3) Empty- the eyes appear as voids, giving the impression that "no one is home". This is the look of depletion, of giving up, and of disconnection from self and the environment.

4) Steely / piercing- the eyes appear focused outwards with an intensity that seems to "look right through" an observer. This is the gaze of hypervigilance and of focusing on individual details. It telegraphs anxiety and distrust.

5) Mirrors- The surface of the eyes appears only as a reflective surface that masks anything beneath it such that an observer is essentially, shut out. The basic message is, "I don't want you to see me."

The plot thickened. I asked Hub if he had noticed. And he had. More research, more information, but all down to us to deal with and try to fumble our way through. At this point the only help he was getting was the hour a week session with the Art Therapist. She realised that his issues were so deep she didn't really do Art Therapy, but she saw the desperation and tried alternative methods to help him. I do think he started to trust her. And as I said it was a session which was actually for him, involved him, and one to one. The therapist did actually think they were making progress. Which was really positive. Sadly we got to the Summer holiday, sessions stopped, and never restarted, as there was a new plan in place, so I don't know whether the progress would have continued. I had to tell him that he wouldn't see her again. So he wasn't happy with me for that. And however great she was, he became one of those ticks in a box for her, a case consigned to her filing cabinet. I expect she thinks of him from time to time, but only as you think of a book you read or film you saw that moved you. It's not your life is it.

Famalamadingdong

We did speak a lot to famalam about our struggles. Granny was a very experienced teacher, and SEN coordinator in her time. I mentioned she had also adopted lots of children. I suppose it gave me some relief to hear that she had never met a child like Boy. She could not work him out. She would say it was like he had depression. It's true it did seem like it, if he was an adult people would be so worried about his demeanour, and they might actually do something to help. You know we wrote to people. Our MP. The Government Adoption Advisor – when there was one. They were so very sympathetic, but all they could do was say that they knew these situations were hard and we were not the only ones faced with such struggles. Great.

Are you thoroughly depressed by now? Sorry about that, you could stop reading I suppose. It sounds like life was one long barrel of crap. And in so many ways it was. But we still tried to cling on to that dream of family life. We did the things famalams do. There were flashes of how it should be. Boy came down to dinner one day dressed as Brian Johnson from AC/DC. Girl wrote and read a poem for Burns Night, Hub killed a haggis. We went to School fairs, and discos. Got kicked out of the safari park for riding bikes in it. Rolled down hills. Grew vegetables. Went to see Santa. Had visits from the tooth fairy (who was very naughty actually). Swam. Fished. Camped. Ate cake. And custard.

There's nuances of normal. Like true British stiff upper-lipped citizens we underplay or down grade many things. The Force ten is a bit windy, the Flu becomes little sniffle, the missing wing mirror is a inconsequential ding. So when you described the tempest raging in your house, as a trifle challenging and people comment that it's normal, to be expected, their age, tiredness, excitement, you want to retort that in fact you fibbed, it's all shite, decorated with a pile of shite. It's meltdowns, it's destruction, it's horrifying, it is definitely not OK. And to tell them I want you to hear me, really hear what I am saying, and then collapse in a big blubbery pile at their feet, for them to pick you up, dust you off and make it all better. But you don't do that. You button up your rigid lip and say no more. Mostly. The times when you think you can try to make people get it, to genuinely give them a glimpse of what lies beneath, are often the moments you regret. Because you change things for them. You may have misplaced your hope, but why should you force them to? Nobody's a total idealist, but why disillusion them as well as yourself? To what end?

My best friend and I didn't speak for three months after a frank exchange of views about being too bothered about the little things, and just accepting that everything was "normal". My wonderful single, childless friend with lots of nephews. She's the one for whom I once wrapped up two live crayfish, affectionately called Ronnie and Reggie, as a Christmas present, and then Hub cooked them for her breakfast. Dudes! We are OK now by the way. You can't lose 40 plus years of naughtiness just like that. And she knows that I know she's a tad weird, and all of the mischief from primary school was her fault anyway. Just saying, in case she is reading this. What I'm getting at is that for many years we had these trusted voices telling us that all was actually OK, even though we knew it wasn't, and the only reason they were doing it was because they cared, and felt that if they said we were doing a marvellous job, and shouldn't feel that we were struggling, that would help. In fact it didn't. It just made me feel like a useless loon.

Life was shall we say, difficult. All those wonderful occasions where memories are made, the simple things in life happened, but in the background there was this big black cloud, of Boy's utter sadness. Around this time we really admitted to ourselves that Boy was out of our control. School reported (thank goodness they were so open) that he had made accusations about us, and said that Hub stuck his fingers in his eyes, and put his hands round his throat. This just made us sad. Really, I don't know if this is a normal situation for parents in this day and age, but you can go on denying accusations, or just accept that making up stories goes with the territory. That thing about thou protest too much kicks in. What's the point? The worst they could do is contact social services! So we did nothing. Hub was to be fair, quite internally devastated and still hasn't forgotten the feeling he had that day. For his bull and bluster he is very gentle, and what Boy said hurt deeply. I still see the lady that Boy spoke to that day, and I feel very paranoid about what she thinks.

Our dear friends, who were local upstanding members of the community, and hugely forthright, decided that they couldn't possibly ever have Boy on their own, just in case he made accusations about them. Well they had a choice. We didn't. But that was one less support. I don't blame them though, people have to do what's right for themselves. Girl took to wearing earmuffs to drown out the constant screaming and wailing. Fair play, and a clever move on her part. Dog mostly still hid under the table when Boy was around, and developed a great line in whole body jelly-like quaking.

I guess then I was at my lowest. I would stay awake too long, because I didn't want tomorrow to come. Joy had done a disappearing act. I couldn't see an end, and sometimes I would think about just driving away. Of course I never did this, I cracked on, we both did, and we went to all the meetings, and tried to be empathetic. Sadly by this stage we were so angry at The SS, we had developed such a mistrust in the system that had promised it would be there for us, we were feeling like incredibly bad people. How could we not do this, why weren't we good enough. We were still waiting for help. Or even for the kind of help we needed to be identified, by someone, who would actually commit themselves. I felt like I was going mad, there was no end in sight, what was the end anyway? It felt like a completely helpless situation. We were at the mercy of other people, who we didn't trust.

It was probably a year and a half after we had cried for help and said we were in a crisis, that they finally applied for funding to go to a proper therapy centre, hundreds of miles away to see one of the best child psychologists in the country. We pushed for this, we said we would go anywhere, any day, any how. We were very lucky to find her, I read about her and she received glowing reports from other professionals and clients alike. So by heck we grabbed that opportunity balls and all. This was for the family DDT which had been discussed with Young Psycholady. Although this was such a huge leap forward, we still had to wait for approval. Young Psycholady went off on surprise maternity leave, which meant that there could be no planning for a replacement, The Apparently Mad Psychologist who had visited before we had chosen Young Psycholady, took on her appointments, and offered us a telephone session. Seeing as she is the only person whose comments I have taken such exception to that I physically leapt out of my chair, and left the room, we said no. Counterproductive. We always talk about Young Psycholady as if she was some kind of genius. But she spent an awfully long time with us and oversaw our demise. She was the one who suggested that should Boy refuse to put his shoes on in the morning we should take him to school shoeless. Never mind how this might affect his self-esteem. What about reinforcing toxic shame? Seeing that you might report the parents to Social Services might you?

So that meant nobody supporting him or us, but we were waiting for the DDT to start, which surely was going to help. And wait we did. For three months to get approval, and then two months for an appointment. The sessions at the trauma centre had been stopped for over six months. It was just us, again. Unless you count the pop psychologist Social Worker. She counted herself as very supportive. Bloody awful time.

So we had a Christmas on our own. Normally we would go abroad, where they really know how to do a Feliz Navidad, or go to family. But we decided that we couldn't subject family to the strain of dealing with Boy. It was one thing him spoiling any occasion we had, but there were five or six other children and the grandparents to think about, and we just couldn't do it. On Christmas day the tantrums and screams began, something about one of the presents. I found Girl sitting in the living room tears streaming down her face because of it. I felt so sorry that day. The turkey got burned, the sprouts were just mushed up green slime. It was just genuinely shit.

We had another couple of months after Christmas where we waited. Really I suppose we were functioning like automatons. I can't remember. There was a glimmer, as we got a date to go to the fabulous DDT place, and they began their conversations on the phone with us, where we were as honest as we could be. We would be getting a session a month. I was called into class a number of times a week, each time to discuss the latest incident. I would stand there waiting, and then get the nod, or the beckon, and my already heavy heart would disappear out of my bum. I would then be regaled with the latest woeful tale of the day. It was clear that Boy was only managing in the class due to the incredible support from the teachers and assistants, who by now, knew him so well. His classmates would call him naughty, which he loved. He disrupted, refused, wet himself. I couldn't stop it, and neither could Boy. And we were really struggling to help him.

SNAFU

As we set off to that first DDT session we were a little apprehensive. In fact that might be the understatement of the century. I remember feeling horrid about it. My husband will say I didn't want to engage from the moment I sat in the car. I did actually, and from my perspective he was quite frankly frightful that day as well. The moment we walked through the door to meet the staff, they took the children to have a play session, I lost control of my emotions, for the first time in public. We always wondered whether part of the problem in accessing help was that we had that stiff upper lip mentality and didn't collapse on the floor in floods. So they assumed we were actually OK. But this day was different, I don't know why. But I couldn't stop, I went over the edge, which was a bit of a shock to them, and me. I wished I had shares in Kleenex. The Proper Child Psychologist in charge instantly realised the crisis we were in, and set about trying to unpick things, and actually understand. It was weird. But it was too late.

We went for I think three more of these sessions and it got progressively worse. I managed mostly to control myself after that first time, but they could see that this famalam had such problems really serious help was needed. They told us we needed to face the fact that we needed to stop trying to be his parents, and start being his carers. I do get what they were trying to say, but we had just spent so long trying to parent him, of course we had, we were not fostering, we had followed all the guidance given, and all of a sudden new experts were saying this was wrong, and he couldn't be parented. It really annoys me when foster carers are called foster parents. They aren't the parents, no matter what has happened to the child. They take the place of the parents in many respects. But they aren't mum and dad. And we were. Their aspirations, their investment, their commitment is arguably different, albeit with all best intentions. It is not always a commitment until death do us part. So how the arse did they expect us to not try to be mum and dad. Remembering that moment on the doorstep of the first foster carers. And remembering how we wondered how we would ever live up to the names mummy and daddy. Well we were now being told that we never would, and never could. Now as I said I get that they were thinking that it would take the pressure off us, and him, if we didn't try so hard. But we had Girl to think about. How were we suddenly supposed to "parent" one of our children and

"care" for the other?? This was starting to make no sense. We were in a big world of poo.

After the initial three month sessions we asked for a meeting to be held with them and The SS. We wanted to get everything in the open. The Proper Child Psychologist had different views on ways forward and put these down in writing to us. Not only did she talk about the non-parenting aim. For the first time we saw in black and white that we might be causing emotional harm to Boy, by allowing him to remain in the situation. By fighting to keep him. Feck me, that is what we had been saying all that time. We needed help to get out of the situation, we knew it was no good for him or Girl or us. But this was in writing, and used the phrase "emotional harm", sirens rang, red lights flashed, alerts were raised in us. Pop Social Worker had recategorized Boy as a Child in Need, she said to enable us to access more services, we royally objected, the next level up was Child Protection. With this new opinion, we felt like we were heading down the road of being accused of child abuse, and we needed to stop this new track and quick. This is where those friends who wouldn't look after him had got to well before we did. Suddenly our family and friends views started to become more understandable.

We called the experts together, Pop Social Worker, her boss, Proper Child Psychologist and her colleague and a four hour meeting was held, at our house, everyone being hugely friendly and jovial. We had three scenarios to discuss. We put it like this.

1. Situation Normal All Fecked Up. Remain as we were. But honestly they said we will definitely, you have our word for it, we swear, support you.

2. Let us look at the residential school option, that was suggested by the other experts, for when he starts secondary. Give us hope, that we can work towards a proper therapeutic option, planned, where we can work towards a situation where he still has and is with, a loving family but it is all managed, and people are helping.

3. Section 20. Which was a spectre that had been raised before but suppressed. A Section 20 arrangement is basically handing over your child voluntarily to the care of The SS, so that they can get support in place, which you are unable to offer. Hopefully with a view to the child returning to you.

So what do you think the upshot was? Option two? Are you having a laugh? Have you ever seen a month of

Sundays? Me neither. The Boss Lady definitely, categorically, infinitely and to the ends of the universe knew for a fact that this would not work. Boarding options were off the table, they did not work. Of all the one cases that she had experienced she knew without a shadow of a doubt that this option was under no circumstances really an option. Nothing to do with finances you understand, it just does not work. Option three? Well hold your horses. Don't have a knee-jerk reaction, this is not necessary, no-one is suggesting that it a good idea. We don't think that there are problems with you per say, and you don't need to go to these extremes. Thou protest too much. But, we pointed, you have made him a Child in Need. You think it's us not him. You want us to change and then everything will be all right? We can't cope, we are in crisis and have been for a very long time. What do you expect us to do? The Boss Lady offered to change Boy's status back to normal from Child in Need, and told us we should give ourselves time to think about what we wanted to do. We shouldn't act on a whim, we would be supported, everything would be lovely and fine if we just held off a bit. Basically eff off and deal with it on your own some more, and come back to us when you have agreed with us. So Option one then. The Fecked Up one.

The one we said and had been saying for some time, was unsustainable and not the healthy option.

Lord Agnew, minister for the school system, welcomed a report commissioned by the Boarding Schools Partnership, in mid-2018 (Boarding School Placements for Vulnerable Children and Young People, 2018) which said "send foster children to boarding schools because it can have a life-changing effect". Oh the blooming irony. That this should be in the press, and the broadsheets at that. On further Inspector Gadget detective work, I find that in December 2017 the government announced the Boarding Schools Partnership to give certain vulnerable children such as those who have been in care the chance to be put forward for bursaries and scholarships to attend "some of the countries best schools". The thing is, we know that Boy was absolutely capable of achieving this on his own, but the absolutely frustrating part about this is that they are still saying that this kind of educational environment can actually be good for these vulnerable children. So we wouldn't have necessarily needed the support of this new government initiative, but we desperately needed the support of the local authority.

Possibly doing it now we might see a change of view. That's now government policy is it? Oh well yes what a good idea The SS has had. It could most certainly keep the family together. Lots of big ticks on their part. But because that one sanctimonious cowbag said in her massive experience of one case that it didn't work, it didn't happen. I cannot tell you how it frustrates me that one opinionated tooth, one more cog in that big SS machine, that makes the wheel turn, can stymie everything you think is right and good as parents, that experts have recommended. Whenever I imagine her voice now, I want to get my tractor out and run over her. To a large extent I will forever hold her responsible for the underselling of a very talented boy. For ensuring that his future academic achievements are limited. For not seeing that boarding could offer stability, space and support. For not seeing the opportunity to give him (and us) the chance to stay together in a different way, and weather the storm. For taking the hope away. Patronising, superior, self-righteous woman. You sit there talking at us, in an ever so softly belittling and faux-supportive manner, occasionally passive aggressive (something I am frequently accused of) whilst underneath your mind is trying to add up the cost, or the responsibility of what we are saying. And then when we've gone, you get your latest minion to stab us in the back. Have I mentioned that I am not fond of this lady? Oh, I don't need to? Good. She to me was the archetypal example of someone who has risen above their talent and now needs to prove herself at every opportunity, not to her serfs, but to her superiors. She seeks pats on the back, she craves the power, and the acknowledgement that she has it. And she cowpats on people like us who dare to challenge. But with Boy not at the centre, issues unresolved and him undersold, it is he and his family who are further traumatised and broken. I don't suppose she will ever think about the damage she caused.

Feck

We did give ourselves time. They walked out the door, and we were livid. It's not that The SS didn't agree with us, it's that they wouldn't even listen and consider all options. Including the option that would enable him to stay with his proper family but give us a practical way forward. The Proper Child Psychologist said that she hoped that in writing what she had written, and in saying what she said, we would give ourselves permission to think what before had been unthinkable. That Boy might be better off somewhere else if we couldn't raise support to ourselves. That maybe we couldn't be together any more, and that that was actually OK, because in care he would get the proper funding for the support he needed, but on a daily basis be cared for by highly skilled therapeutic "carers", not just parents who "cared".

Probably three weeks later we were in the car, just me and Hub, coming back from a session with our therapist, and we decided we couldn't go on. The SS had offered nothing by way of support, and just done absolutely nothing. So that first option was still unsustainable, option 2 had been discounted. It was like there had been a rising wave of thinking in a different way, and we were losing the fight. It made sense what the Proper Child Psychologist said, if all of the things could be brought to bear in a different way then that was a no brainer. There was none of that fecking support that was promised to us, nothing changed, and if it couldn't at that crisis point, it made us believe that nothing would. We had to take Option three. Section 20. We called Pop Social Worker and told her to sort out whatever she had to do, and that we would requesting to place our Boy back in their care.

What happens next is a bit strange. The SS make arrangements to find a placement for the child, whilst you are still carrying on. We were advised that until we knew what and where we should not say anything to him. We were coming up to the Summer holidays, and so we were forced to let him carry on as if he was going back to school in September, and pretend nothing was occurring, all the time, and I mean all the time, day and night wrestling our consciences about what we were doing to him.

They wanted to ask our family if they would take him. What the actual hell? They said no. In two impassioned letters from our parents to The SS they independently told them that they had struggled to deal with him as grandparents, they were in their 70s and quite frankly could not comprehend why such a question would be asked. They absolutely supported us 100%. There is a thing called an FGC, I think it stand for a Family Group Conference. The SS wanted one. They wanted our wider family and friends to sit round a table and be asked whether they would be willing to take on this child. In those letters to the Pop Social Worker, our parents said things like "I understand why (Boy) behaves as he does, but dealing with it is difficult. To be called to a conference and have to actually reject someone you love is not only unthinkable, but unbelievable" and "We are shocked that, given the degree of specialist help (Boy) needs, as identified by professionals, it should even be considered that family members or friends would be able to provide that degree of expertise and commitment", "We trust that you will now do you best to help (Boy) as we have all tried to do for the past four years". I have to say that those letters written by both our families independently of us, or each other were striking in their similarity, and really expressed the feelings that had gone unsaid for so long, they made us feel rather humbled. They were sent directly to the social worker from them, so there could be no doubt as to their origin.

It transpires that Pop Social Worker was herself questioned by another big cheese as to whether "*you* are in contact with any of the family members or friends, (as opposed to the parents being in contact). That is, is there anyone you can contact and talk to – it is often the case that parents say there isn't anyone because of their own feelings about not being able to look after a child when, in fact, there is". This, from another even more important SS Leader, I think basically adequately demonstrates the views coming from above. Let's be clear, we felt no trust, no positive relationship, no team, and no support. This thing about the parents can't look after the child, they are incompetent, it is their fault, we will lump them pretty much in with the child's birth parents who neglected and traumatised him, and don't trust them as far as we can throw them. The Pop Social Worker did I think, forward on those letters as evidence. I don't know. It's not recorded. Which is sad when you think of the agony that our parents must have gone through to write them. We have brought a lot of sadness to their doors haven't we?

I found a letter we wrote to our friends, which says "*We have as you know had various interventions, assessments and advice given, thrown, imposed upon us in relation to how Boy should be parented, in response to our cry for access to the help and support which was supposedly on offer. At first it was too little, now it is too late. We are all very damaged and we no longer have any fight left in us to ensure that support for Boy. Going forwards we are going to continue to do our very best to try to help the child that we can and desperately hope that someone who already has the skills and experience will be found to help the other.*

We are currently in a situation where Social Services are yet again procrastinating but we are developing a "line to take" which we hope that all those who know Boy will take so that the transition can be made as painless as possible, and we also hope that we can give Boy the chance to say some farewells, and that people will contribute to a memory box for him to keep. He does not know as it would be entirely inappropriate without a concrete plan in place to introduce this to him, but there is necessarily a deadline of for arrangements to be made because without one, Social Services are unable to function.

Boy's teacher said to us today that he wishes those advising how to care for Boy could have walked in his shoes for a week in trying to help him, and we feel exactly the same and we dare say you do too. We could never have anticipated this happening with all the hope at the beginning, the emotional investment, but for the last four years we have been failing Boy because we did not know how to care for him and cater for his complex needs, and opinion is still divided but we cannot allow this to continue for all our sakes". Our friends responded by telling us that they had got to the point where they were going to tell us to do what we had decided to do anyway. Which was comforting in a way, but rather shows how people hold back from telling you the truth, because it hurts.

This was unbelievable. We couldn't get our heads round the fact we had made this decision and we probably thought we knew more than we did. But we still had to try to fight for the best for him. We gave them a deadline as we said to our friends, on the advice of a professional who told us that in a similar situation she had dealt with where deadlines were flexible, the child was still with the parents after six months. We couldn't let this happen. We basically told The SS that we would be leaving the country (only on holiday, we were coming back), and so they had better get a placement sorted. Apparently though, there were no foster carers of the level needed with capacity in the entire country. Amazing, it was fine to leave us complete useless chuffing amateurs with no support, but once the responsibility was to rest with The SS, the requirement and qualifications for carers was sky high.

The Proper Child Psychologist had said that Boy needed an experienced therapeutic foster placement, where he was the only one. And all of a sudden, literally one week before he went, a place was found. They had no other children. Good. That was about all that was good. They were too young (in their 20s). This would be their first ever foster placement. We expressed our concerns, but basically were told this was the only option. The Proper Child Psychologist had said that we should take Boy to do goodbyes to important people in preparation. The last minute arrangements meant that everything was dropped by our family and friends to achieve this. We sat the children down and explained what was going to happen. She was a bit teary. He just asked if he could take his duvet.

The next week was like a living nightmare. We did the length and breadth of the country taking him to see people, they had all been asked to contribute to a memory box for him, and they all put so much beautiful thought into something very special to give to him for later in his life, to remember (this very important box of his which has subsequently been misplaced). He marched into each house, waited for his gift and couldn't wait to leave. With a smile he told the one boy from school who had stuck by him that he wouldn't be seeing him again, so get used to it. It was the most bizarre experience. We had tried to get some information on the people he would be staying with. The SS had it, but unfortunately Pop Social Worker was part time, and it was her day off, and nobody else could be bothered to try to access it for us. So we had nothing to show him.

Three days later, Pop Social Worker turned up to pick him up to go to these new people. She had brought with her Bored Social Worker, remember the one we chased away. This was a precautionary measure in case he kicked off in the car! Hub buckled him into his seat, facing empty eyes from Boy. The three of them drove off and no one looked back. I think at that moment the absence of attachment became very real for Hub. Girl stood in the hall. We all hugged. Including Dog.

Definitely, Maybe...

We have come to the conclusion now that we don't fit in a box. Nobody can work out how to deal with us. Often, and I am generalising hugely here, as one does, a child might be in foster care, having been taken away by The SS rather than through a joint decision. We were treated then and now as if our child had been removed from our care as a default setting. At the start we were allowed what they call "contact" sessions, once a week. We had to go to a contact centre. An anonymous, spartan, slightly grubby feeling Council place. This was a converted house in the middle of a load of lived-in houses opposite a big shop in town. I have no idea what normally went on there, but you had to buzz to be let in, and out, and so could only go in working hours. It felt like a bit of a walk of shame as you went up the garden path and waited while someone demanded to know why you were there. We were also alert to the fact that we might be arriving at the same time as Boy and his foster carer, who we hadn't met, and this might be a bit awkward for him, them and us. Once we were allowed in we were accompanied to a magnolia room, with not a lot in it, where we would await his arrival on tenterhooks, after which the Social Worker would leave the adjoining door to the next room open. Some guff about it being so that she could help Boy. I have to say the location and the audience did not help make our first visits with him a positive experience. It was like visiting time in a prison.

They wanted him to come back to the local school. We said not on your nelly. Really what goes through their heads? How could it possibly be sensible to send a boy to a school where he would see his sister who was still with his parents, the parents with whom he no longer lives, and face all the obvious questions from peers. And to drive for 45 minutes to get him there everyday. We put our feet down, and they managed for once to see our point of view, and there started the struggle to find him a school place. Apparently this was very difficult, I don't know why. Oh, actually I do. Because there was no plan. I guess it was around two months before he began, at the nearest school to where they were. It can't have been that difficult can it then? By this stage the young foster carer, who was very optimistic and judging by her posts on social media rather misguided in what she might be able to achieve, was I believe, in reading the reports, driven to distraction, with

him at home all the time, so she was receiving very regular respite and support.

There's a system called "Virtual School" which in my words is supposed to exist to help children in and from care, and make sure that they get the best education continuity, particularly because their lives can be transient. So did this system kick in? Virtually. So virtually in fact that nothing happened, to keep him on track. When he got back to school they decided that he was so far below expectations, that the previous school must have made a mistake. In fact they blamed them. Our marvellous SENCo had offered to visit the new place to help to settle him in, and to give them some of her hard earned knowledge about this little boy, and pass on some wisdom about all the strategies they had tried, from specialist training they had secured, some of which worked, to help him engage. Unfortunately The SS could not sort this out, and the new school rather conceitedly decided that they didn't need this help and carried on in their own way. Trying all the same methods, failing, taking him back to square one. They gave him a full-time teaching assistant. Brillliant idea. He began to rely on her for everything, and strangely couldn't work independently any more. He started to become angry and somewhat fisty by all accounts. But of course this was our fault.

We finally managed to get an agreement to directly speak to the foster carers to arrange to see him, and actually go somewhere else, somewhere other than the "institution", somewhere more natural. Our meetings with Boy didn't feel nice. We felt that we couldn't really engage, but we persevered. We thought it was inevitable that it would be uncomfortable, as his emotions would be riding high, but we started to notice his behaviour changing, and him being even more out of control. We were pushing for the promised support to begin, but we were told that they wanted to see how he was in a different environment, (an assumption being that his issues being purely environmental of course) and get him settled first. Some more words of wisdom from Pop Social Worker with the psychology doctorate (not).

The foster carers did take him to see the old child psychologist, but reportedly found it rather hard, who are they kidding? They decided that they probably wouldn't do that again. No one from Social Services was going to drive him 150 miles, so that was the end of that. The art therapy couldn't be restarted even though it was in the same town. All the funding fought for was given up, seemingly without a second thought, maybe because it came from the wrong piggybank. Pop Social Worker was full of it though. The different methods of caring they were using was definitely bearing fruit, he was really settling in. They removed boundaries, allowing him to express himself. And express himself he did. He ignored the Cockeyed Optimist lady foster carer, would not speak to her, bounced off their four walls and the ceiling, and went a bit feral. Oh, and then Boy accused the fella of being red faced, angry, shouty and scary.

In case you are wondering about Girl, after he drove off into the sunset with Pop Social Worker, and we had crashed to earth, we left the country. With some trepidation I have to say. All of a sudden we were three (and Dog makes three and a half). We had no idea how Girl would react, but thought we should escape to where we could be a unit, like at the very beginning but a new formation, and this time having removed, and stamped on our rose-tinted spectacles. Abroad, we did the things we normally did, but quieter and calmer. Dog reappeared, once more full of vim and vigour. She revelled in everything, including the cowpats. She was herself. And I knew this because when she is a happy hound she genuinely walks sideways. Looking back I remember the feeling of waking up in the morning without the horrendous pressure that would descend, and I guess we relaxed.

Girl was brilliant. She was cheerful with her unique spin on life, that somehow pervades everything. She had our attention, we stuck to the boundaries, but everybody was visibly chilled. From that fateful Friday she has never once said she wanted it to go back, and believe me we watched for the signs of distress. The brother that life had to revolve around, the constant being since she was born, was not by her side any more. But she started to blossom, and when people saw her afterwards they all said so. Things got normal I suppose. We always say that all of a sudden she went from that 20% of our time, to 100%, and for her that felt good. Until she did something she shouldn't have, and then she couldn't hide any more, or blame anyone else. But this was fine. This was how it should be. I can tell you we had challenges with her, but who doesn't with a pre-pubescent female? I was one once and will reluctantly admit I was somewhat feisty. Is that strong enough Mother?

Nearing the six months mark, these emergency, temporary foster carers decided they couldn't go on. They handed in their notice. I gather that caring for Boy had put such a strain on them that it had contributed to the lady's illness, and they could not cope any longer. Despite this being a job, and having weekly respite, and a lot of support from their manager, and The SS, they just couldn't do it. Fair enough, I got it. The SS had rather stretched the definition of temporary though, and we were somewhat relieved, as we felt that the boundary-less strategies were having a more detrimental effect all round. They were not the therapeutic carers the expert had said he needed. We had our first Local Authority Care Review with an Independent Reviewing Officer. I am not going to describe her, because I suspect you would find me awfully rude, suffice to say I could paint a Picasso-like picture without much effort due to her unique style, which with my sartorial incompetence is saying a lot.

Thank You, Next...

At some point when the topic got difficult the Cockeyed Optimist's husband and fellow new foster carer got a bit overwhelmed, burst into tears and had to leave the room. We sat there in a rather uncomfortable silence for a second before cracking on with business. Later on, the Indescribable Reviewing Officer told us that we should put in an official complaint about their conduct. Pardonnez-moi? If you believe there is a problem Ms full of "I am here to hold the Local Authority to account", because I am very scary, then that is up to you to report it. Not us, who nobody would give the time of day to. Anyway the foster carers quit. Don't get me wrong, they were really nice people, and in another life I can imagine having a beer with them. But their idealistic image of what it would be like was shattered. They thought they were there to save him, and they couldn't. They posted photos on social media with this poor abandoned child, and talked about the fun they were having. But they couldn't do it. It wasn't fun, and he got worse. They say he abused their dog.

So the search for a place started again, and we all waited. Over Christmas we waited. All this time we tried to push a little, but the new Social Worker (I forgot to tell you he had a new one, and I am now very confused because I also can hardly remember their faces now) said that no way would he be placed at that time of year, too emotive, and so the foster carers entered a limbo that I didn't envy. They knew there was to be an end, but not when. Eventually they did what we had done, and gave an absolute date to The SS. This galvanised them. The search was stepped up in good time, sorry wrong, actually it was something like 48 hours before he moved, that being the absolute deadline that had to be put in place, again. The SS decided they had to look at private agencies. It's the cost you see. To place a child with an agency costs the local authority a fortune, and someone has to justify this expenditure. So maybe this is why they hold off as long as possible. Again, they knew what was in their system ages before they decided to go externally. But there are procedures you know.

The day before the notice period was up, I spoke to Number two Forgettable Social Worker. So Pop Social Worker was still Girl's and now we were on our second, third, what ever for him. The Three Musketeers. Except none of them seemed to speak to the other one. Number two Forgettable Social Worker didn't know him, or us. Except on paper, and believe me it did not read well. Everything still pointed to the fact that we couldn't do it, and wouldn't accept that, despite receiving no effing help. Bastards. I know this because we put in a formal request for information spouting the Data Protection Act later on, to receive reams of records, emails and reports, where we were portrayed as obstructive, and angry. Quite frankly offensive, and we said so. Anyhow the day before the definite end of placement I phoned Number two Forgettable Social Worker and I asked her what was going to happen with Boy. She said he was moving the next day. I asked where to. She said she didn't know but he was definitely moving as she was going to pick him up. I wanted to know where he would go with no place to go, and was basically told a children's home. I was so horrified, I started to think about telling her to fuck it and bring him back, whatever the consequences. At 5pm that day I got a phone call. A placement had been found. 300 miles away. With some therapeutic and utterly, and handily, proper suitable foster carers, from a private agency "dahn sahf". Did I agree to it? I had no details, there weren't any. What could I do, the choice was stark.

Either he came home, went to this placement, or went into some form of children's home. I said yes.

So he moved again. We didn't know where to, or who with, but he went. A week frigging later we got details. We set about trying to arrange to see him. It was not easy. In the end only Hub was able to go on the only day available. We discovered Hub had been working about ten minutes away from where they lived, which could have been awkward! He had a very difficult meeting with the new carers. They told Hub they were a bit concerned that it was just him and not Girl too, because they weren't sure that was allowed. I can only imagine what the foxtrot they had been told. Hub spent probably one of the most peculiar hour's McDonald's has seen. He came home in a right old state. Boy had told him that he knew why he was living there, and that was because we abused him. This was new, and language we had never heard or expected to hear from him. And it must have been very awkward for the carers if that was the sort of thing he was saying, to then meet one of the people he was talking about, and leave Boy with him in a fast food establishment. I would have been secretly looking through the windows if I were them. I was devastated when Hub got back, I just wanted our Boy to somehow trust us to have done the right thing.

We have subsequently found out that when Boy arrived there, all his clothes did not fit, he had no possessions with him, he began by leaping on the furniture, he would eat with his hands, he swore, and was incredibly rude, slept under the bed, wet himself. What would you think about the parents of such a child? I know what I would believe. So God only knows what these foster carers must have thought. The evidence was leaping up and down before their eyes. And they did have experience of other children. I am sure they believed that the state of him must have been all down to us, not to do with the recent foster carers letting him express himself. I do believe that this thought exists today as I will explain in a bit. Remember that Pop Social Worker had said all Boy's issues were environmental, and she was the one overseeing the case so that's what went down in writing. Since he had been handed over to various Forgettable Social Workers, and no-one has time, because time is money, I don't think anyone genuinely invested.

His behaviour in terms of his mental state was the same when he arrived with his new carers, if not worse. And it was very distressing for us to see, so it must have felt the same for them. And him. He was out of control. He was agitated, edgy, having tantrums, punchy, and all the same issues were presenting. And now he was socially a nightmare. Now I have asked myself so many times, did we (and the pre-us Foster Carers) make him keep a lid on this, did we not understand that he needed to express this side of himself in order to get past it? Was it his kind of baby behaviour that he had never had a chance to show when he was first on this earth? Well it probably was, but a nine year old needs to also understand that they are not the only one in society, that there is a big world they need to fit into, and to allow a nine year old to eat with their hands, or to jump on chairs, or swear, and to not see that their clothes do not fit, and allow them to hurt you, as a free form of expression, surely this cannot be the right way either. Certainly these new foster carers did not think so. And we were glad. They clearly stated that they had firm boundaries on what was acceptable, and his behaviour was not. We agreed, not directly, as we were now apparently not supposed to talk to them, but through the latest social worker. Yes dears, he had another one. I can't remember her to be honest, she was so momentary, she was full of ideas, and went to see him, and them, and she agreed wholeheartedly with us about everything. We had hopes. But it didn't help with the blame game. The first foster carers have disappeared into the ether. No-one mentions them. That talk by the Authority of making a formal complaint about them never came to anything. All forgotten. To what end they thought we should complain, I have no idea. If they thought there were such serious issues then surely the complaint should be official, where is the formal safeguarding? No-one was going to listen to another whine from us moaning Minnies. So we did not make a complaint as advised, but we made our thoughts clear. We thought.

Number three Forgettable Social Worker reported that the new carer had said she was going to make Boy into a "chav" to help him fit in. Whether she genuinely said that I have no idea. I also don't really know why the Social Worker thought it was amusing to tell me this. I have just looked up what CHAV means. Charming! I'm glad there's an acronym, but why would anyone be proud to say that?! I thought it was an insult? I was horrified. FFS, Taking into account the child's background is supposed to help them make sense of their lives previously. Not to deny their past. The new carers were told nothing about us. When we saw Boy he told us that the other kids had told him he was too posh, so that needed to change. What could we say? He was in survival mode again. His hair changed, his clothes changed, his accent changed, he developed a swagger and an attitude. In the space of a couple of months. But this must have been ok because the Social Worker didn't comment. We weren't going to start fighting over things like this, he also seemed pleased with his transformation (at least on the surface), and we were certainly not going to be critical. We knew him, and we knew what a survivor he was, and if this was what it took to help him feel he fitted then we would just live with it.

We had said so many times that his behaviour when toddlery was just that, distressing, but not dangerous. We feared that unless he got the right support as he got older and bigger, these displays would change, and become something different. What we heard about then, somewhat confirmed our fears. He hadn't been excluded, yet, his new school reported he had been on the brink. He hadn't seriously hurt anyone, or himself, yet. What lay in wait, we did not know, but we did know that without looking back they can't look forward. Know where you've come from to help decide where you are going. It was a massively worrying time for him, and those around him, but they failed to see it. At that time nobody was left who knew him, or us. This worried us greatly. But no-one sought our opinion, thoughts, knowledge or experience of him, seemingly preferring to deal with issues as they cropped up. We felt for the foster carers, as all they had to go on was the fact that a troubled, and struggling child with no belongings had been dropped on them, with a distressing story surrounding him(we know not which version).

We struggled then to establish a routine of contact with Boy. Our emails and phone calls went unanswered, everything was last minute. We met Number three Forgettable Social Worker twice in six months. She did not know him, and everyone was left to their own devices. I am still glad that the carers own social worker seemed very supportive, I think they had known each other a long time. This might help it work. We were still told in writing when we actually got any info (we had asked for a monthly note about how he was doing) that he was doing brilliantly, although verbally when we did see the carers at the contact sessions, that he had to be restrained regularly and the school suggested that any other school would have excluded him by now due to his violent behaviour. Depends on your definition of brilliant really doesn't it?

The Law Is An Ass

There's a vital point with a Section 20 placement. You are asked to sign a delegated authority sheet, or complete a process to say what The SS can and can't do. You remain the parents, you have full parental responsibility, which can only be removed with a Care Order, which can share that responsibility with The SS. Unfortunately when we were asked to do this the local authority computers were not working, so Pop Social Worker had made her own copy up, with about three key points, to say that we agreed, of course, for practical day to day decisions to be made, but that was it. We were not going to hand them any more than that anyway, not until they could prove to us that they would use the responsibility responsibly. If you see what I mean. He was still our son and we needed to ensure that everyone acted in his best interests. This meant that we needed to be informed of what was going on. It appears that this form was misplaced, and did not exist any more. Which means that The SS were really supposed to revert to us being responsible for every decision about Boy (including haircuts!). More on this later. Suffice to say they seemed to overlook this, and so many decisions were made without any authority it was shocking. What was worse was that we were just ignored.

In this process you have six monthly reviews with that Indescribable Reviewing Officer, appointed as she had explained the first time, to effectively hold the local authority to account. Six months after he went into care she phoned us, and told us she was dismayed at how no support had been put in place for Boy, and that would be the thrust of her dealings with The SS. Remember, she told us that we should make a formal complaint against the Cockeyed Optimist Foster Carers, and she also said that in all her years of experience Boy was the strangest child she had ever met.

At the review she held with us six months after that, still with no support in place she was a little more circumspect. She made recommendations that a Care Order should be pursued. We categorically stated that until we believed that The SS were acting in his best interests we would do our best to contest this. You have a tightrope to walk. You can actually be accused of abandoning your child if you are not careful. In one of the last proper conversations I had with the Indescribable Reviewing Officer she told me that although the new foster carers seemed to be a long term solution for Boy, they had not actually agreed, and their agency would not agree to them having him long-term under a Section 20. They were rather bloody stuck. The IRO therefore pronounced that a care order was necessary. I pointed out that they would have to meet the legal thresholds for this, and that we did not consent. She suggested that there would therefore be a stalemate. Correct I said.

This talk of threshold criteria is a bit officious, but it is a fact that they simply cannot get a care order in every case. The rules are that

A court may only make a care order or supervision order if it is satisfied—

(a)that the child concerned is suffering, or is likely to suffer, significant harm; and

(b)that the harm, or likelihood of harm, is attributable to—

(i)the care given to the child, or likely to be given to him if the order were not made, not being what it would be reasonable to expect a parent to give to him; or

(ii)the child's being beyond parental control.

(Section 31(2) of The Childrens Act 1989)

To get a Care Order and take parental responsibility the Local Authority has to evidence that it is because the child is at risk of harm. How is this fair on either the adoptive parents who already feel like failures and end up basically being blamed on paper for putting the child they tried to protect at risk of harm, or the child themselves who will grow up believing that those people failed to look after them properly. Apparently there is case law now which says that there can be a no blame care order but this seems to have escaped our SS.

They planned a meeting. A statutory meeting. A "disruption" meeting. Because that is what this situation is called. A disruption. Not a breakdown of adoption. No it is a disruption. What kind of politically correct jargon is that? Yes it's bloody disruptive to everyone concerned, but to the adopters and their adopted children everything has broken down. "Hello, hello, is that the 4th emergency service? Yes, I am on the hard shoulder of the M1 and my vehicle is experiencing disruption". I will stand corrected but in our case on the original SS record we are probably down as a successful adoption, whatever chaos has ensued.

At this meeting, many do gooders gather together to try to work out what went wrong, and learn lessons for the future. We weren't exactly invited. I mean what did we know about what had gone wrong? Actually I lie, we were invited-ish. For an hour. Of an eight hour meeting. How the eff were they going to discuss what happened honestly without us there? And what in God's name were the righteous twits going to say if we were not listening? Don't forget Boy will be able to access all his records one day, and we were damn sure going to try to get these right. So we just told them we were coming for the entire day. And we did. I put on a smart shirt, not too businessy, but smart enough, Hub got his blazer out.

During proceedings, we were placed on one side of a 30 place table arrangement, everyone else sat on the other. We were not offered coffee, but at least we had a seat. And so it began. The dissection of a little life. How did he get where he is today? It was chaired by a rather biggish cheese. Who was so incredibly nice all day. Turns out he was the one who managed to leave us without any information to give to Boy about where he was going when he was first placed under a Section 20, because his staff were off, and he couldn't work the system. He emailed to say he was leaving that day we needed help from him, at 5.01pm precisely, clearly demonstrating to us his willingness to work massively past his going home time. This meant that we went without the information that was vital to helping Boy to come to terms over the weekend with what was happening. Needless to say we didn't therefore have a very grand opinion of this cheesy chap, Mr Smarm if you like. And probably he didn't think too highly of us either.

We had wanted to be really prepared for this Disruption meeting. First of all I asked Mr Google about it. No other bugger was going to tell us what would happen, and Mr G had been my faithful friend ever since we first met, and I needed to know why coconuts are hairy, how to get goose fat out of cowboy boots, or where I could purchase glycerine in France without being gendarmed for substance misuse. I knew he would definitely tell me the truth. Mr G said it would be stressful, because we would feel fingers of suspicion pointed at us, and that our own laundry would be fully on display. We had even gone to the lengths of putting in a Subject Access Request to the Local Authority. In case you wondered, this is where you ask organisations to supply you with all the personal "data" they hold on you. And they have to respond. If not they get their wrists slapped by the Information Commissioner himself. And that hurts.

We just felt that there was so much that had gone on and been talked about behind the scenes, and it's not funny, but people don't talk any more, they email. And emails are data. It was a shame that we didn't get the results (all 500 pages) until a week after the disruption meeting, after exactly 40 days. They now have 30 days to respond by the way. If we had had the info before the meeting we might have had a thing or two more to say. In the emails we were sent, we discovered that aforementioned Mr Smarm was involved in many of the delays in finding Boy a placement, due to resourcing issues, and Pop Social Worker disgraced herself in our eyes, with some of the opinions she expressed to others in the Authority about us, effectively putting on record that it was all our fault. But at the time, at the meeting, we had none of this information, so we dealt with what we did know.

Before the meeting and trying to understand for myself what had gone so terribly wrong, I had also found some interesting academic research into attachment disorders and I emailed the author. I told them that I was "particularly interested in his idea that the diagnosis of attachment disorder might become all-encompassing when looking at an adopted child and therefore might mask underlying issues such as ADHD." I think I just wanted them to help me with a more articulate way of expressing my thoughts. I can come across as a burbler, sorry if you have already noticed that. The person responded, cautiously, as they had never met me, and I might go and quote them. It's a dangerous game, putting pen to paper. I will quote them but I'm not going to reference it. They said one question I could pose to the local authority was "*in what way is the foster care you proposed going to be a better and more stable solution for this child's needs, that could not be met with appropriate, and as yet untried, support within the adoptive family?*" and that "*the issues around caring for him might not reside wholly within your capacity to parent him, given other professional carers have potentially also had difficulties caring for him, but rather that there may remain unmet needs within him that continue to challenge parenting effectively.*" They also said that "*with the best will in the world, there are people unwittingly denying children the opportunity to be seen as individuals, not attachment based stereotypes. But if you suggest that, you tap into a very sensitive criticism of their (genuine) commitment to these children. They genuinely believe in the truth of their attachment, or trauma, or foetal alcohol or whatever the label is, formulation. It's strange and you can end up hitting a brick wall.*"

I have to say I wished I had come across them before. Their comment about being seen as critical of that commitment that these social workers have to the children they come across, struck a nerve. I would never doubt that these people are ultimately doing the job because in their way they care deeply, and believe that some if not all are there for altruistic reasons. They juggle life balls in an unwieldy and ultimately increasingly resource-led circus, and deal with people at their lowest points. At this point however nobody would believe that I could empathise with them, and anyway I didn't need to do that, it wasn't my job. It was confidence boosting to hear from someone who was clearly blessed with a big brain (being a published academic) who could put into better words what I would like to say. I emailed them and said I was very grateful for their thoughtful and considered response, because I really was.

On the meeting day our SS dragged in the first Local Authority to talk about how Boy came to be in the care system. Although not Obsessed Social Worker, the one who was really really really fond of the children. I expect she has moved on finding the job too emotion-inducing. The someone else they brought in couldn't explain why it took the first three years Boy to enter the Care System when he was suffering knowingly. Then came discussions over how the nice Custard Cream Social Worker had made mistakes, in the handover to us, which was too quick and not detailed enough. Well she wasn't there to defend herself was she, so that was taken as fact.

Posh Social Worker, was there and was kind about us, and said she couldn't see it coming, and reminded them how she had tried to push for more support for us before we adopted the children and how she had recommended we allow him to change his name The wonderful SENCo came, and I think she was more nervous than us. She very articulately made her points though, and when asked three times what the school could have done better, each time she told Mr Smarm, nothing. With confidence. And she was right. They could not have been more caring, more supportive, and more like a port in a storm for us, when we were adrift. She told them how worried she had been for not only Boy, being once upon a time his actual teacher, and actually knowing him, but also for us, and told them in her opinion that we were good parents, that had basically been shat on by them. She didn't actually use that word by the way. Not only that she told them that in order to get some help for Boy the school had dipped into its own coffers to kick start some therapy. I don't recall anyone making any eye contact with her or us at that point, as they shuffled their very important paper work around, Mr Smarm cleared his throat, thanked and dismissed her.

They brought in Apparently Mad Psychologist and Young Psycholady (who had talked to us not Boy), both of whom were very supportive of us. The Proper Child Psychologist was connected by Skype, and was sort of trying to get across her point that in her opinion without targeted therapy Boy would continue to go through his cyclical behaviour of rejection of anyone who came close to being close. But what did she know, they were The SS and they made the rules... Bored Social Worker was conspicuous by her absence, her name hardly mentioned. Weird. Pop Social Worker was there though, by God she was there. And she spouted some guff about us and our situation. At this point she knew that we were about to know most of the negative crap she had written whilst at the same time pretending to be so understanding to us, when we received all the emails from our Subject Access Request.

She told the assembled deities how she had arranged the final meeting before Boy was placed under Section 20, due to her concerns, at which point Hub nearly went through the ceiling. I think he stopped short of actually saying the word "liar", but he suggested she might be massaging the truth a little to suit her story. Concerns? If she had concerns she would certainly have done something about it instead of sitting on our sofa drinking effing tea for a year and a half. She told the truth, half the truth, and not very much of the truth. I understood the merits of voodoo dolls at that point. Her boss, remember the Cowpatting one, well she actually did not stick up for her at all, her silence very revealing to us, but probably nobody else noticed. It was then agreed that in fact she did not arrange any meeting, we did, and they did not express concerns, we did. Manipulative buggeress. I guess that was pretty much the end of our beautiful friendship. In fact despite the fact that she remains Girl's social worker, she did not speak to us in any way shape or form for the next nine months. Her loss.

It was like some kind of disturbing dissection that day, and ended with everyone leaving after being dismissed by Mr Smarm, and walking down the corridors not saying a word. We departed The SS Headquarters gasping for coffee, got in the car and drove off, not quite silently, but you know when you have so much to say that anything you do say just seems pathetic. Well it was one of those moments. I felt like a deflated bouncy hopper. A sad, slightly misshapen blobby interpretation of something that used to be so springy and fun. And then I did the school run. Because life goes on. I stood there in the school playground looking around at all human life, little and big, and thought, why couldn't it just be like that.

The report that finally came out of that meeting is probably now consigned to being yesterday's chip paper. To us it was full of the usual inaccuracies. Bullshite. Not that anyone was ever going to learn a lesson from all the high fallooting spouting off they did that day, because any concerns that they raised about their own ways of doing things in Boy's "case", were soothed by the fact that they had apparently made changes in all of those areas already, so this shouldn't happen again to any other child in their authority ever. A rip-roaring rooting tooting waste of time. A classic bureaucratic hoop that had to be jumped through, to make sure there was no comeback on The SS. Isn't it great that they judged themselves not to have failed, those not there were blamed (thank goodness we went) and if there had been a little blip it was before their time, and things had changed now anyway. Yes, great for Boy, who was at the centre of these shenanigans. Anyway this was looking backwards, and the need was to look forwards. One of the most important recommendations said the report, was to "avoid over-optimism". God forbid one should think positively.

You know when dealing with authorities on things, you probably attempt to speak their language. You don't write emotional emails and sit in meetings telling them how much you love someone. That's not what they are interested in is it? That human side is forgotten. We were talking about our son, our little boy, but to them it was just another case file.

Not Fine

So Boy had now been in his placement, with these second carers for nearly a year. In that time, we struggled to see him, and he had two new social workers. The Third Musketeer Number Three Forgettable Social Worker had been replaced by what appeared to be an anti-social worker. She was agency. She was a very well put together, manicured and precise lady. She had spoken directly to us approximately twice. We were not necessary to her. I think the normal SS struggled with these weirdo agency people, and I didn't understand their place in the Social Work stratosphere, they certainly believed they are at the top of the social work nobility. She came with a laptop, and a phone and everything, very 21st century. She was proper with it. Unless you asked her a question, want a response, and expected anything to be forthcoming. Hub said she embodied everything of Dickens' Circumlocution Office (I agreed with him after I'd secretly looked up this wry reference). Then there was some malware in the system and response is not possible and you basically got the blue screen of death, the ever spinning wheel of non-responsiveness.

The carers still knew nothing about us. They didn't know anything about Boy's life with us, or before. They didn't know where he had lived, what he did, what he achieved, where he went on holiday, what he was interested in. I think they were encouraged to think about the here and now, put the past in the past. According to anything we could glean from The SS, the foster carers, and he, were encouraged to think that his life started when he arrived with them.

Under the eye of the authority's Virtually Useless School a meeting was arranged to talk about secondary schools. All meetings for us now were done by phone (we were not encouraged to drive the 300 miles to attend). From the muffled voices on the end of the line we ascertained that his school had been chosen. Er, but, hang on, we thought, we don't know anything about this, and the School have only known him 3 months, and the Social Worker is 300 miles away, and and and. But we couldn't argue, we didn't genuinely have a say, and it would have looked churlish to suggest that the massive school most local to the carers might be the right one, or it might not. We had to try to trust that this was right.

I do think that because there was a complete arse-up of understanding surrounding the parental responsibility thing, there was huge confusion from all sides over who could, or should do what. So The SS and the foster carers made all the decisions about Boy. We were not given an opportunity to contribute. They told us they were going on a day trip abroad, so asked us for his passport. We pointed out that this would require permission, and a letter of agreement. Why weren't the sodding SS sorting this out? We handed his passport over for this trip, and told The SS to sort a frigging letter. Otherwise they might turn up to cross the sea and be accused of kidnapping. They didn't go in the end, but kept his passport. We were then told they were going abroad again, and that Boy was very excited. We were not asked. So we asked The SS about who had given the permission or signed the authority for this one. We were told that if we didn't want him to go, then they would have to cancel his booking, and tell him he was staying at home because we wouldn't let him go. Oh. The point is that there is a simple process, just that no-one was interested in following it.

Around Christmas we kind of had to fight to see Boy. It turns out the foster carers had gone away and he was in respite, not that the Anti-Social Worker thought it necessary to tell us, even though it was absolutely necessary to tell us. The thing is that because the foster carers were assuming that we were being told, and I guess were doing things how they had done them before, and nobody was passing on anything from us, this was not going well. Finally I think the message got across that this was a special time of year, and so important for the children to see each other, and met them. Our family had all contributed to a huge box of kit from his favourite football team, a team which I had always objected to, having my own long home-grown allegiance, but a team he had supported since before he came to us. Family had done this the Christmas before, but all the kit had disappeared, along with lots of his other belonging (apart from the ones that didn't fit). The foster carers said this was what he really wanted, more blooming football kit! We handed it over. They had arranged nothing for Girl from him, so she was a bit peeved. After Christmas he told us that he had been given a computer games console, and that this was the best gift ever and he was obsessed with it. Did you get the football stuff we asked. Er, yes, er, thanks, came the response.

Anti Social Worker, his social worker, who we had met twice in six months, lived hundreds of miles away from him, and us. We couldn't work out when she was seeing him. Or what she was doing. If she didn't see him, and left everyone to their own devices, it didn't mean it was all better. Turns out after 6 months still no progress had been made on any aspect of his life, no therapy, no CAMHS help. He was underperforming at school. He was erratic and becoming violent. They suggested anger management sessions six months before (treat the symptoms not the cause…) Hadn't happened. No progress made on any long-term plan. No progress made on getting everyone together to try to talk about issues. Somehow it was like treading water, badly. I'm not waving you eejit, I'm drowning!?

I think we probably pissed everyone off whenever they heard from us, because if we would just stop pushing, then they could tick some boxes, rather than have to do any work. With the Anti-Social Worker in hiding, and this new notion of not being directly told anything, we had no idea what Boy was doing, or who with. Should we have given up? Should we have stopped stressing about it, accept that we did our best to fight for him and have to hand him over completely. Well that was an option. But we feared that no one had thought about the fact that we remain his parents for ever. Foster carers are short temporary or long temporary, but temporary nevertheless.

They would not encourage the relationship with his sister. We give up, it all stops, his life is totally in their hands.

His sister carried on as before. Lively, likeable, happy, grumpy, intelligent Girl. Who still needed support. And still had Pop Social Worker in order to facilitate the support. We hadn't seen or spoken to her since that debacle of a disruption meeting months before. I didn't really care. I never wanted to see her again. Sadly we needed her. Separate problem, but indicative of The SS attitude. Where once we were talked about as difficult, and failing to do right by a child, the remaining enfant is left in our care, with no question about how we do it. Strange.

We couldn't work out why we were so side-lined in everything since boy was in foster care, never mind the opinions that Pop Psychologist Social Worker had perpetuated about us. Legally we retained parental responsibility. Yet no one felt the need to ask us anything or indeed tell us anything. How it works as I mentioned, with a Section 20, is that the Local Authority never has parental responsibility, but the parents are asked to delegate aspects of it, for practical reasons. And of course we would not say no, as long as it was in his best interests, to anything. But we are not asked about school choices, we are not told about incidents, we are told that he is going on a foreign holiday, which actually legally requires written authorisation. Do you remember I spoke about the need to sign over certain responsibilities, and the computers being broken on that day? Well, it turns out that a huge assumption had been made that we had signed some form with the Pop lady, which delegates authority for decisions from allowing haircuts (apparently haircuts are a hugely emotive issue) to big decisions like schooling, and medical care. We had repeatedly asked for a copy of this form which we allegedly saw, to prove it did not exist more than anything. Surprise surprise it never materialised. Because it didn't chuffing exist that is why.

Something else that did not materialise was any direct communication from Anti-Social Worker. She was, it appeared, a mistress of disguise. We became increasingly concerned, and it was at that point we came to that conclusion that the way he appeared when moved to his second placement (as in completely wild, with no clothes the right size, and with such concerning behaviour) was put down to us by everyone, even though he had been away from us for a year or more. We are all human, often we can only believe what we see, and it's hard to shake first impressions, so despite time passing and us offering to support the foster carers, because we understood how hard it must have been, we think they retained that impression, that we were neglectful parents. All the Social Workers did not help. Boy spins a yarn, as a defence mechanism, and it is believed. The foster carers admitted that they struggled with him, and that he simply could not tell the truth, and no doubt he said some hurtful things about them, or the previous carers. But none of this is in writing.

We decided to act, and contacted the new boss man who we had been told about, to try to get some action, and get something done about the lack of delegated authority, to not accept no answer, so that everyone knew where they stood, and we could all work together properly. He did some digging and found that despite all the assumptions that they had a signed document, they didn't. He was incredulous then. In his own words they had failed (again this was not in writing), but at least someone else seemed to see how concerning this was.

We put in another one of those Subject Access requests. Not to cause trouble, but we felt that there must be more information floating around that we did not have. Please don't think that I don't know what it is like to receive one of these pesky requests. I have been at the other end of it, and when I asked staff to please send me the data they held on a particular person, they said something along the lines of, does that include the email I just sent calling them a … (word I would never use)? Er, well in theory yes. I have produced reams and reams of data to give to people, overdoing it, so that they would know that we had gone to lengths to provide the information. For goodness sake the Council has a bunch of people whose only job is to do these things, the Data Protection Team or whatever it's called. They have to do it, it is the law. And I understand the frustration of vexatious requests. But frankly if they are going to store information about people, with new-fangled technology it is easily done, then those people ought to have the right to see it. In our case, we knew that there were these discussions taking place that we were not, and definitely should have been, party to, and that the whole story was not being told, as nothing seemed to fit together. In over a year there had been no progress and no communication with us, to speak of. This was the whole point, to identify and get him the support he needs. Surely at that point people could understand that it was not environmental, that he really needed help.

Meetings Blooming Meetings

So we had a meeting. Don't look so surprised, although I know we hadn't had one in eons. The new boss man turned out to be somewhat unusual and on the surface unconventional, underneath I think he is quite similar to the rest of The SS. We had to take Girl with us. It was the frigging school holibobs. Meeting was in The SS Headquarters, which is probably rather daunting for some, and I think is gopping. A beautiful old building, massive, but filled with glass boxes where people can work and meet in full view of everyone else. The reception lady gave us a number on a stick, to take to the seating area, like in a restaurant. I felt like one of the unwashed masses, if you get my drift. As the boss ambled past and said hello, Girl looked up at him and forgot to do the poker face. Her surprise was evident. Later she said it was something to do with his beard and his clothes. Not his piercings mind you. We entered one of the glass boxes, her outside in the foyer where we could see her, nose in her latest Harry Potter, saying we would be twenty minutes.

One and a half hours later we emerged. At the meeting with Mr Unusual he said that no way would the threshold for a care order be met, and he would not recommend that course of action. Well I never, he was the only one who said that to us, in a genuinely caring way. The previous person to say it was Pop Psychologist Social Worker at the first Independent Review meeting after he had gone into care. I recall she remarked to the IRO that she would be contacting "Legal" but didn't think it would reach the threshold. The way she said it was not caring, in fact it sounded like a threat. At that time I didn't have a scooby what she was referring to. I can assure you I do now!

Let me summarise the rest of the meeting. I assumed we would be presented with the missing authority form and sign bits to say other people could make decisions about our son, but we actually managed to arrange another meeting with others included, to discuss it. Mr Unusual spent much of the meeting drawing in breath, sometimes head in hands, and me waiting to see when and if he would exhale. Hub reckons he was on the back foot, panicking, he admitted liability, their fault (as I pointed out to Hub though, not in writing). A lot of "you have very right to...", "you are not being unreasonable…", "you are clearly intelligent and articulate…", "nobody could say you were not patient…". Lots of that. Platitudes? Maybe. But yet again we stated the case for our position, we told him that we were treated like abusive parents, like second class citizens, and that there was friction. He told us that Boy was hearing voices. Thanks for not telling us that before, only vaguely important. Oh, and the small fact that the foster carers had told them they were potentially throwing in the towel three months ago. Again thanks for the information about that "wobble" as he called it. Every traumatised child needs wobbly people. He told us this unimportant piece of information after announcing that he was aware we had put in for a Subject Access Request, and probably we might be quite surprised (and not in a good way) at some of the things this revealed (now why would that be I asked myself, unless people haven't been telling us everything). So yes, that surprised us. Well done.

He didn't have any answers, except to say we needed another meeting. He sighed. We shook hands and left. May I say at this point I actually rather liked this unusual chap. He did genuinely seem to try to see the big picture, and all points of view, and his job was very challenging, caught between all those Social Workers and the top dogs. His I am genuinely more hip than a hipster head was genuinely on the line.

We ruminated on what he had to say, or not say as it were. We had pretty much decided that to have another meeting including all "parties", where we all decided what parental responsibility we as parents would delegate, was not really how we wanted to do this. We started to think that when it came to that particular aspect, that we wanted to make the decisions on what we needed to be told about, by ourselves, and then everyone else should be told this is the decision. That's all we wanted, to be told the facts, and to have some input into big decisions. We were not going to get our big spanner out and throw it into the works. We absolutely got that for day to day stuff it is really important that there were no hold ups. You can't function otherwise. And the foster carers needed freedom, and to be trusted, to make those decisions. So we told Mr Unusual that we wanted to decide only with him what to delegate, he agreed and in another overlong session the form was done. And he was going to send it to anyone who needed it. Good, one step forward.

Anyway, we then got the email with the results of our subject request. "All" the information or data as they call it, that the Authority holds on you. "All" fitted into two emails. All two hundred pages of it, spanning a year, and countless people's correspondence about you and your family. Two emails. Absolute bollocky bollocks. Transpires that either The SS are not very good at keeping records or there might have been some stuff missing. I know this because I have the stuff myself. The emails I received from whichever number social worker we were on, mentioning whichever document was saved to whichever system. However what we did receive almost floored us. I read snippets out to Hub as he was driving on the motorway, and he nearly made a new slip road. If you will indulge me for a minute… in an email from the Indescribable Reviewing Officer to the latest social worker… "I am aware that parents are not aware that the placement is ending and its only time before the carers let this slip"! Let this slip! Let this slip!! My effing eff. So that's OK is it? No it effing isn't. Hub used the word "duplicitous". In what sense is that OK? This was a month after the foster carers had said they could not cope, and three months before we were actually told about that "wobble".

Probably there are people out there who must wonder what we thought gave us the right to argue that we should have a say, because we gave him up. This subject is so difficult and emotive and although I can talk about it all as I do, in my wandering way, I will probably never come to terms with what happened. But what I do know, and my answer to anybody who wondered, is that we promised to take care of Boy, and we would do anything in our power to keep that promise, and make sure everybody else took care of him too. I'm asking myself whether we were so caught up in the whole frigging palaver and feeling so offended by the turd-flinging, that we should have forced ourselves to stop and let The SS just get on with it. At the end of the day Boy was never going to live with us again, that was clear, however devoted we were to him. I don't think we could have done that to Girl (or him). And the very eminent Child Psychologist had said basically that should never happen, which is why the going into care was supposed to be carefully orchestrated. Why did we seem to be causing such a ruckus all the time? It only served to make us out to be a pair of loons. But even now looking back, I think that we couldn't have lived with ourselves if we had not challenged and questioned. We felt awful already, and had we not done everything in our power to try to get the right people and support for Boy, then we couldn't look him in the eye and said we did our best. We hurt ourselves in the process, but we had to keep fighting. This whole parental responsibility thing was so important to us, because we had gone over the rudiments of a Section 20 with a fine tooth comb, and we believed we would be able to carry on being there and fighting his cause. Probably didn't help that we had placed too much trust in people already, and put our family at the mercy of others, and in our eyes this trust had been broken so many times, that now we didn't trust anyone. Although we did try.

You're Just Too Darn Posh

I really thought that by this stage we would be able to look back and know the best thing had been done, to know that we had managed to protect him. But unfortunately I couldn't. We had another meeting with the Indescribable Reviewing Officer, and thought that no doubt the recommendations that hadn't been followed would be discussed, and more timescales would be put forward. And that the meeting we had had with Mr Unusual would have helped to make some progress somehow. We just wanted to see Boy supported properly but we had lost complete confidence in anyone actually having his interests at heart. I read a cautionary tale about having to be very careful about what you do with a Section 20 placement. They were talking about that ability of The SS to accuse you of abandonment of your child. We know that we took that route for the right reasons, but everything can get twisted and you end up feeling like you are balancing on a tightrope. We refused to give up and let him be at the total mercy of The SS, because of our mistrust of them. But then it is suggested that by not allowing them to take total control you are putting a spanner in the works. Does that mean you are preventing them from acting in his best interests. We didn't think so. But then we wouldn't would we?

Of joy of joys for this IRO meeting. The night before Hub asked me whether I was worrying about it, and I decided I wasn't. This review is supposed to look at the "case" and make sure things were going in the right direction. We had to fill in a form with our views, which by eck we did. The Indescribable Reviewing Officer knew that we knew what she had been saying, because she had supplied her emails to us through our request for information. Remember she had said that they mustn't let slip the fact that the foster carers had given notice? And the fact that she had suggested we would reach a stalemate if we didn't give in to a Care Order. And the fact that she had told us last time that we must email her with any concerns, which we had done and by and large had no response. You remember that we hadn't seen or heard from Anti-Social Worker in six months? Well I was in a weird way looking forward to hearing what they had to say about the fact that raising concerns over the complete lack of progress had led to … well … a complete lack of progress. Plus I had decided to smartly out-shoe the

Indescribable one, which meant that I felt quite confident, because I always could look at my feet. Great.

I cannot put in a nutshell the farce that ensued. It was worthy of some kind of Two Ronnies Sketch. At one point she said that what we were asking for was not normal. We thought that asking for some communication over big issues, seemed perfectly reasonable. They hadn't taken our child away, and we were interested in seeing the best outcome for him. She changed her mind and said our situation was not unusual. When she commented that we could always ask the Anti-Social Worker, I spoke before my polite filter kicked in and proclaimed "she doesn't ever respond!" Then I remembered she was sitting next to me, and looked at her, with one of those rueful sorry but it's true expressions. She did not respond. The IRO mooted the idea of setting up six weekly "Team Around the Child" (TAC) meetings to try and get everybody talking. Oh crap I thought, back to the meeting train. She suggested that this way when things were not happening we would know about it, and be able to flag it up. That is not our job though, and we said as much. And we also said that we had already done this many times in the last six months, telling her directly. But apparently all she can do is make the relevant people aware, and only recommend they might wish to possibly, maybe, potentially actually do something. If they then didn't? Well there is not a lot she can do. So what is the point of her?

We were asking for a quick note on what had been going on from the foster carers, once a month before we saw Boy, just so we could understand what he had been up to, or whether there were any achievements, or issues to be aware of. When we see him the last thing he wants is twenty questions about stuff, he was eleven for goodness sake. And also there was his propensity to somewhat exaggerate. Apparently though according to the IRO putting this down in writing is rather onerous and not a normal thing for foster carers to have to do. We then find from the Anti-Social worker that she gets a weekly report from them anyway. Me not understand. All we wanted was a few lines to help us all. So would it be difficult for us to somehow see the information that they already had. It does appear so, because it wasn't normal, and God forbid one should think outside the box.

Lots of things that should have been hugely important were discussed at this meeting. We asked them why therapy had not been started. We were asked by the IRO what sort of therapy he should have. How the feck should we know. If they have read the reports that they spent a fortune on then that might help. One minute she was suggesting that lack of therapy had contributed to this well good placement potentially breaking down, then saying once a week music therapy was enough. Speaking of placement breakdown we were told that the foster carers had not actually given notice. This is not what the emails that were bandied around unbeknown to us said. "Yes, well they didn't give notice, they just said they wanted to end the placement". That's the same thing you daft cowbag. I didn't say that by the way, I only thought it.

Then came the most jaw-droppingly incredible thing I had heard for a long time, and it has rather made my memory of everything that followed a little hazy. We were suggesting that the reason that we felt a little friction between us and the foster carers, and why it seemed that they didn't feel they wanted to communicate with us in a normal and more positive way, was possibly due to the way we had been portrayed to them originally, and that no work had been done to help Boy understand his identity and "life story". Therefore there were a lot of misunderstandings that no-one was helping to sort out. The IRO proceeded to say that this was definitely not the case. They truly, honestly liked us, but the problem was that we were middle class and they were working class!!! Well I never. I hope there is someone out there who agrees that this is an appropriate thing to say. See what I mean … Two Ronnies … "I look up to him because he is upper class, but I look down on him because he is lower class…" At that point I lost the will to live, left my own body on the chair and floated off into a better place. We needed to end this crap. We have to write this down because nobody else will. When we got home we ate lots of Haribos, and sat in the kitchen somewhat agog. I rang my mother. Hub rang his. We passed on the agogness. The inability to make any sense of it lasted until around 11pm, when after some medicinal alcohol on a school night we downloaded our brains onto a piece of paper, where it was even less understandable.

Once we got over our disbelief at what had been said (and a wee hangover) we tried to start to understand where we were. Quite apart from all our peeps reaction to the middle class thing, which without exception met with absolute and utter amazeballs disbelief, we wanted to try to move on a bit, and we knew we needed to establish some kind of better communication with the foster carers, and somehow get this all working for Boy. It had become clear that using different ways to communicate, from gently trying to persuade, to shouting our bloody heads off, from cajoling to being rather direct and forthright, none of it worked. The IRO had told us to tell her when we were having problems, so we did. After two of her review meetings where she had basically fobbed us off, by saying actually she couldn't force anyone to do anything, we really were at the stage where she was being as useful to Boy and us as a cocoa related hot beverage making vessel. We could wait until she sent her report out, no doubt receiving it late, then read it again with incredulity, or we could do something. We decided that we needed to move forwards, not backwards, we would attend the meetings, try to be constructive and gently try to improve the relationship with the foster carers, although of course the IRO said it didn't need improving, they liked us and respected us, despite us being up ourselves. We had to do something, the negativity and frustration of it didn't just stop when we weren't dealing with it, it pervaded your life, and still would appear all of a sudden in the most surprising way.

I had an email from an old colleague, who I was working with when we were going through the approval process. She had never met the children who were the result, but had fond memories of our time together, and wondered how we were getting along… I hadn't told her what had happened, she was going through her own crisis and I didn't want to burden her, so now I kind of had to go through it all in a nutshell for her. How strong you are she said, how positive. I disabused her of that notion. Not strong, not positive, mostly feel like a shit.

All Wobbly

We had suggested, at the instigation of one of the three musketeers type Social Workers six months worth of dates for contact with Boy. Everyone agreed that this was a good strategy, no SS involvement in the plan, just an agreement between us and them so we could put the dates in our diaries and not have to always be worrying about finding a mutually convenient date. Of course even with dates planned in advance people have difficulties, but it was a starter for ten. We'd struggled to communicate, and see Boy around Christmas and New Year, we now know that the foster carers were "wobbling" at that time, so we kind of understood that it must have been difficult. We tried to put ourselves in their shoes over that period. The last thing you want if you are having doubts is to be hassled or even reminded of the problem, you don't want to admit you've got a problem and we probably represented the problem to them and they certainly were not going to admit to us that life was difficult. And I can categorically say that it must have been very hard. I understood the pressure and stress and challenges that came with caring for Boy. And even though someone from The SS is there to supervise you as a foster carer, and you do get some respite, at the end of the day you are living it. Sometimes 24 hours a day. And that is tough I know.

But then there was another mix-up. Over the dates that had been in the diary for some time. Boy was in put in respite again, so he couldn't see us. Twice. The SS were not helping to promote Boy's contact with Girl. Because the Anti-Social Worker had gone to ground no information was being passed on. We were however dismayed that the foster carers hadn't told us, even though we had directly tried to confirm we were seeing Boy. I can't make an excuse for that. They just didn't respond, until they did. I guess they felt mightily pissed off too. We were challenging and annoying. So they sent us a snotagram, which I won't go into, but the accusatory content was very upsetting. We complained. Mr Unusual agreed it was not acceptable, and that we should expect an apology. That's how adversarial it had become. And this was so wrong. Although the time we had spent with Boy seemed to be getting easier for him, and he was genuinely laughing and more relaxed, somehow all the "grown-ups" around him were locking horns. We just felt more crap and useless. We couldn't do anything, and now it was clear that the fruitful and positive relationship we had hoped to pursue with the foster carers was struggling even more. There were no proper delegations, lots of misunderstandings, and a complete lack of clarity for anyone. And you do start to wonder whether it is literally you, because you are just horrid.

Having time to reflect on this development didn't help. That rumination. I think that it ate away at us more than we knew. The black cloud of confusion and feelings of frustration that were there all the time, the fact that we considered ourselves to constantly be at war, and at the mercy of The SS, and constantly felt like we were wrong, when all we were trying to do was the right thing by and for Boy and not let him get lost, would sometimes override everything. When one of life's normal little challenges happened, you lost your car keys, Dog vommed over the duvet, you got a tax demand from the Italian Government for your deceased uncle, your tooth cracked, your kitchen flooded, you got flu, it was like the end of the world, plague, pestilence. If my boiled egg exploded, I imagined it as just another test for me. I used to look up sometimes and ask what exactly I had done, to be surrounded by all this crap. I had long conversations with my Buddhist friend about the virtues of his beliefs. I marvelled at his calm and gentle exterior and wondered how I could be more like that.

May I also say, at this point, Girl, who we believed was on more of an even keel, without the day to day intensity of her relationship with Boy, was having her own issues. Due in part, no doubt to her age, that bridge between little and big, between child and adult, with the confusion in her mind over wanting to still be five and also wanting to be a teenager. Wanting cuddles and comfort and on the other hand being embarrassed about bodies, feelings, and on the cusp of understanding some of those more grown up issues of relationships. Wanting to be protected but also wanting you to stop the things that used to make her hoot, "being ridiculous" wiggling your bottom in public. She struggled with peer relationships, her self-defence mechanisms were strong, she would never relinquish control, and this spilled over into bossiness, upset, and also the spinning of incredible yarns, just so that your story was more dramatic and more interesting than anyone else's.

The Headteacher rang us one day to say that she had been telling odd stories about people, at school. He was a very pragmatic man, thank God, and wanted to work with us, and for her. But it was distressing, and one story in particular brought home to me the real lifelong struggles that taking on these children would bring to your door. And that there was nothing you could do. I wanted to roll with it, but it took me weeks to chill about it. I guess what helped was talking to her teacher about another story she had told, in front of her, when she admitted she had made up a vital part so as not to embarrass herself. She is an enigma that is for sure. I just held on to the belief that we had brought her up well and she understood right and wrong, and we just had to keep reinforcing that. It was hard though, she was going through her things and we had the enduring Boy stuff.

There was a point when naively I believed that I would just be their mum. Not that I knew what that would mean, but I didn't think that after seven years I would still feel as floundery as I did on the first day I met them. And that I would feel now that I didn't really know them at all. Not deep down. I would never really know what was next. I could control external influences but not the internal ones. That's where Boy had such difficulties. Inside he had been and still was a whirling dervish of emotions and challenges. His own skin would probably never be comfortable to him.

Ruminate we did. And we kind of decided that this farce had to end somehow. Basically we felt that we were constantly being prevented from doing our duty as parents to Boy, and the sense of frustration that this caused and the constant battles to try to hold people to their word, and to account and move things forward were just agonising. You know sometimes I tried to put myself in somebody else's shoes and think about us from the outside. All I ever came up with was that we must be a right old pair of shits, and when you have been feeling that for such a long time, you get a bit fed up of it. They couldn't love him like us, but we needed to allow ourselves to believe they could care for him.

He Said, She Said…

We sent a message to Mr Unusual, who after six weeks had still, to our knowledge, not sent out the agreed delegation form, so still no-one knew where they stood, which put us in a difficult position, as still no-one got the point that legally we held full parental responsibility. We asked to talk about a new way forwards. We were not specific but in our minds we were intending to tell them to take us to court, to do what the IRO had told us they needed to do. Let a judge judge. We did get some advice from a renowned legal chap about this. We had no confidence in The SS to do the right thing, but surely a person of law could look at the situation and say what they felt was the right thing to do. And we would stick to that. Whatever they said. And The SS would have to as well.

We had resisted a Care Order, because we felt that we needed to have parental influence over Boy's welfare, at least until he was really settled. We cared about him as a person not just as another case. But we were worn down. We had fought our little bottoms off to try to make the things that they said they could do, happen. But when they didn't, when he had no therapy, when he had no life story, when we were stopped from seeing him, when we were covertly blamed for his state of mind, there was always an excuse, or a new reason, that was only reasoned after the event. We had no influence, we were just thorns in their sides, and they as a collective seemed to believe that they knew what was right, far more than we did. They didn't quite poopoo the thoughts of all the professionals who had given their views, but they cherry picked the necessary bits and made it fit their reality, there were so many versions of the "truth". The legal beagle had said that we should consider letting it go to court, because then The SS would be forced legally to behave in a certain way, whether or not it was the way we thought was best. And when he said that, it kind of allowed us to think that maybe it was time to allow someone else to make decisions. Hence the message to Monsieur Unusual.

Slight spanner was that two weeks after sending the message we had no acknowledgement that we even existed any more, and this slightly frustrated us. We were trying to move things on. Then Hub had a phone call from the Indescribable Reviewing Officer. We were in the office, and he took himself into the next room. I still heard every word as she caused his blood to boil. She backtracked on everything that had been discussed, she denied, deviated and disputed. She blamed me for not allowing them to consider the option of Boy remaining at home, but going to a residential school in the week. Apparently she recalled Hub telling her I couldn't cope with that. Interestingly I had found an email from that time where we say that they had made that decision. Suggesting that this had actually still been an option six months after he had left us was without doubt, nuts. She kept asking what therapy we wanted for Boy, and he kept saying it was not our place to say, it never had been, we just wanted them to look at the suggestions that had been made before by professionals and that we had never been able to get in place. For f's sake, in the time he had been gone we could almost have qualified as psychologists, then maybe we could say as professionals what was needed, but we hadn't obviously, so we couldn't.

She was now saying that he definitely needed to be settled in a placement before any therapy began. Again. Excuse me, three things: he was in a settled place with us when the wheels came off the wagon the first time; surely at a time of being unsettled a traumatised child needs therapy more than ever; and also who the f are you to decide that? The conversation between Hub and the Indescribable ended rather abruptly. Apparently we were to receive another phone call the next day from the Anti Social Worker and Mr Unusual, to discuss our thoughts. So she would speak to us after that. We emailed the Indescribable and told her what we thought in writing. Including a little bit about her thoughts on social class barriers. It probably didn't help. She emailed us back and said we were wrong. We emailed back and told her we had very different recollections of events that we could back up with the written evidence. Or we might have said she was not doing her job properly without quite using those words. We also asked if she had sent her report out from the last meeting within timescales, then where the frig was it? According to the IRO Handbook (Department for Children, Schools and Families), a work of fiction that probably wouldn't get on Richard and Judy's Summer Reading List, but is statutory guidance, her report should be sent within a certain timescale, which had sadly passed. When you have written what you consider is a good email, that will provoke a reaction, the act of pressing send is like hitting the red nuclear button, and that is what we did.

Five days later we received the report, with a lovely message explaining that unfortunately they had technical issues which is why it was late. Funny because that was what they said last time. Maybe they need to speak to the technical department. Although these things are sent in the post, which doesn't strike me as too technical, so maybe it was actually Royal Mail's fault, or our letterbox. Or Mr Sodding Nobody.

I sat and read the damn thing. Previous reports of these reviews had borne no relation to the actual event, and seeing as I had actually been at the meetings, as had Hub, and we began to think that we were suffering from folie a deux, some form of shared madness. But this would be very unusual, so I was very interested to see how the plot in this one developed. In all honesty it didn't. It was 12 pages of nothingness. Nothing had happened apparently and not a lot was going to happen unless you read between the lines. It talked about the "wobble" that had occurred months back, where the placement was in danger of ending. But anyway they had decided to keep him so that was OK. Child at centre of everything? I think not. Of course there was no explanation of why in the four months after they stopped wobbling, none of the recommendations had come to fruition. I do not know why we weren't told, but this was a classic example of nothing being shared. Parental responsibility? I think not.

Boy was angry at us, said the report, didn't want to see us, but wanted to see Girl on his own. No. I cannot begin to express what a fallacy this was. When we were allowed to see him he seemed pleased to see us, and her, and when he talked in not so glowing terms about what his carers were like, we took it with a pinch of salt. He sought physical contact, sometimes too much. They didn't know, and didn't appear to want to know. We knew that his defence mechanisms meant that he would say what he thought you wanted to hear. So if he had told the Indescribable lady that we were horrid, this was a natural thing for him to do. He was canny, a survivor, he knew what she was there for. If we had reported the comments he made to us about the physical restraint and anger from his carers, would that have redressed the balance? Probably not, and we were not getting into the game of flinging that sort of mud. Anyway, the Indescribable Reviewing Officer used the comments about him not wanting to see us, but to see his sister without us, and what a brilliant idea that wasn't. Let the children be on their own and you can deal with the fallout. But can you do that after you have made sure that the parental responsibility we have delegated has actually been looked at, because I really do not want to be blamed for an incidence of fratricide. I even managed to avoid that with my own big little brother, although even at age 40 I came close.

A new idea also not discussed with us at the meeting, was mooted in the report. Due to tensions between us and the foster carers, perhaps Boy could be brought to contact by an "independent person". Well there you go. We were under the mistaken belief that we needed to sort out the communication problems and help Boy to see meeting us as a positive experience, and indeed for the people surrounding him to be able to talk to each other. She didn't go as far as to suggest that this "independent person" could oversee the contact, but I would have liked her to try to suggest it. There was no goddamn way that was happening. I was certainly not going to give over Girl to a member of The SS. No bollocking way. You know, at no point had anyone suggested that we posed a risk to Boy or Girl, but all this stuff about him thinking we hated him, we "abused" him, it was now all in writing. Where was this going? If I credit the Indescribable one with being intelligent enough to have a masterplan, then I might think this was calculating. This on top of the fact that we had missed a telephone meeting about education, because we bizarrely hadn't got the email with joining instructions to the telephone conference (yes, it really is that swept up). I sound paranoid, but God it just made us bristle even more. And made us even more convinced that we needed to change things.

Having gone unacknowledged for two weeks our urgent request for a meeting finally resulted in a phone call. Apparently Mr Unusual rather unconventionally had no idea of what was going to befall him on a given day so never made a plan. After two weeks the Anti-Social Worker phoned and asked if we could meet the next day. Er. No. Point here was that we were expected to drop everything and be at their beckon call. And we had jobs. Which I don't actually think they knew. We once tried a meeting in our office to see whether that might make the penny drop, but I think they thought it was our house, and we were just a bit odd living in a white box with lots of wires everywhere. Anyhoo, we arranged the meeting for a week later, and in a way this actually allowed us to contemplate what we were about to do. In the meantime we had another contact session with Boy.

So we'd read the report about tension between us and the foster carers, and how it might be better instead of trying to look at why there might be some difficulties, if a "independent" person brought Boy along to see us…something to think about. I had thought about this, and the fact that it was an hour and a half's drive to the appointed meeting place, and that this would be an added tension for him, if he was picked up and driven by someone else, and the fact that nobody had mentioned this to us. And then the day before seeing him, Hub gets a phone call. Sadly, both foster carers are not well good, but unwell and therefore unable to bring Boy, but luckily a Foster Care agency person could bring him. How interesting. He told us she was the "Ceptionist". From where I do not know, could have been the local builders merchants for all I knew.

So this lady turned up with him. He was OK. We did the things we usually did. He was what can only be described as hyper-competitive. He challenged Girl, told us he was the best at everything, swore, burped, sat down to eat in a café, stood up, wandered. We gently asked about his thoughts on things, wondered aloud about why we might have seen it written that he was angry with us. This he denied, but said "I didn't like how you treated me". Girl sat listening, with those big eyes, and said "but you got more piggy backs". I asked him what he meant by that, and he didn't want to talk about it, so that conversation ended. On the way home Girl said she knew "he didn't want to live with us", and was genuinely upset. She couldn't remember specifics, that was just a feeling I suppose. We were in that Catch 22, where we didn't really know how to respond. This all served to really make us sure that we needed to do something differently.

So we had parental responsibility, yet we couldn't fulfil any aspect of it. The SS were not informing us of anything, not one little wiener, no provision was being made for Boy in terms of therapy, we were being cast as anti-the world. Yet ultimately we were responsible if anything went wrong. Also the constant battling was so tiring. The solicitor had said we needed to get in front of a judge who could make a decision on what was best, and we had come round to that. He may be right, we didn't believe The SS knew their derrieres from anything else. If it didn't fit in a box, they would make it go in one way or another. They clearly thought we were deranged. So we told them that. When we finally met with them, Mr Unusual and the Anti-Social Worker sat there, and we had a lovely discussion over the current state of affairs for an hour. And then we told them what we really thought, and what we were going to do. That floored Mr Unusual. And again he understood and nodded sagely. Just after the Anti-Social Worker showed us an email from a nurse who apparently had seen Boy for one of The SS MOT's that children in care have to have, and who he had confided in that we were "not nice people", and the only reason he put up with seeing us was because he wanted to make sure his sister was safe. For crying out loud.

Despite the report from the nurse, we left that meeting feeling a bit better, having told the right people the right thing. And then we crafted our letter to The SS Management to say that in reality we were left with no choice, we were being prevented from fulfilling our parental responsibilities and therefore we all needed to stand in front of a judge who would make the right decision. We got a response in a few days. Along the lines of we will respond to your "lengthy" letter by the end of next month, but please bear in mind that everybody will be going on holiday soon, so we can't say for sure. Please wait, you are on hold, someone will be with you shortly, this is a busy time, all our operators are engaged.

It's Uncle Fester

Whilst we waited for a response to our letter, we had another contact session. We chased it. We asked for confirmation it was happening, the social worker asked on our behalf, because of course we were not allowed to communicate directly, due to our middle classedness, causing intimidation. Yes, yes of course it was happening, and the notes from the social worker suggested he was doing well, as usual.

Turns out it wasn't going that well and there was an issue with the suggested secondary school, that we had thought might be too big and unprepared for him, in that they had decided not to take him, because he needed specialist provision, but no worries they just happened to have such a provision lined up. This revelation came on the day before the last day of his primary education after there had been a "robust transition" to secondary in place for him. What effing choice did we have? We told them, because they had to ask, because we are the parents, that we felt that he needed to start some form of secondary education in the September, but that top priority should be given to the referral that had been made to some paediatrician (again, because don't forget we already did that, and were sent away with the proverbial flea, because he was adopted and it was all down to The SS to sort him out). And that if that investigation led to a diagnosis then fine, but to put him in a box that we didn't know if he would fit, could shape his life for his entire education, and then forever.

So that was a bit shocking. But apparently we were not allowed to mention this to Boy. Someone else was going to do that. So in the meantime they were going to let him believe he would be starting as he thought at the secondary with everyone else. Bollocks.

And bollocks was what we thought when we actually saw him the day after. He arrived with some geezer. Girl said "look it's Uncle Fester", and whilst I don't ordinarily entertain name-calling, the resemblance was remarkable, and the comment brought a little humour to an odd situation. Boy had been driven all that way with some bloke, who we did not know, who handed him over to us, not knowing who we were either. So having been handed over Boy proceeded to behave in an utterly bizarre fashion. He wouldn't make eye contact. He mumbled and muttered. He confronted. He challenged. He prodded and poked his sister. He was not interested in the football we had brought along. He wandered off. Anything to not be with us. It was a strange experience. After the previous positive occasions with him, this was so backward. How this boy was related to the one described in the pre-contact notes I do not know. We did that thing, Girl got upset, asked him what was wrong, he said nothing, we gently told him that if he had said that he didn't want to see us, that was OK, but if he hadn't then he needed to know that people were very confused. In for a penny and all that. It was awkward, and quite frankly unpleasant. We took him back to the appointed meeting place, handed him back to Uncle Fester and departed.

You can guess. We asked. What the Eff was going on? Did the fact that this was mentioned in the Indescribable Reviewing Officer report mean that this was now a fact? There have been communication difficulties, so they shouldn't now communicate? Perhaps he should be brought by an "independent person", costing The SS overtime. Perhaps the foster carers were poorly the first time a stranger brought him. Perhaps the second time something went on. But this is not how a discussion works. And surely a child in the care of The SS should not be brought to contact by some unnamed person with no notice, even to the Social Worker, and just handed over. FFS, what stupid game was this, where was the duty of care eh?

Whilst all this palaver was happening, Girl continued to be herself. Mr Unusual had said to me in one of the meetings we managed to have with him that he hadn't yet received the things for Boy from me that he was waiting for. These things consisted of what is termed "life story" work. We had received when we adopted the children, some documents put together by experts in these matters to be gone through with them when the time was right. Well quite frankly I thought the time would never be right to show the children that crap. At five years old you couldn't read to a child about the fact that their "tummy mummy" (not a term we ever used) took recreational drugs and drank too much alcohol, and for a nine year old, the document was so childishly written it was patronising. We made sure that the children were told everything in an age appropriate way. The fact that Boy recoiled from anyone who had certain physical features, made it very difficult to ever show him photos of his birth father. And so I had kept the documents and photos safe, intending to show them when I as their mother knew it was the right time.

With Boy going back into care, I still had all their documents, and there was no sodding way I was going to give these to some faceless Social Worker to go through with him without me. Some agency Social Worker would not have spent time finding out the facts, and understanding Boy's history, and no way would they be able to do justice to the time he was with us. So I still had the stuff. But I got it out of the attic, and looked at it, to make sure I could be confident in what I thought. I was. And I left the things in a safe place. Not the attic. And not so safe I discovered, that Girl couldn't see an interesting new thing and have a quick look! Well she sat on that information for a few days, and then just happened to mention that she had seen something, and wondered about it. Seen some photos of her birth mother, and told me exactly what she thought. And went off on one, in great detail, about all the stuff she had read. Not that she had spent a long time looking at it mind you, she had just glanced at it. Yes OK darling! So we had some chats. Nothing she didn't already know. No questions she hadn't already asked and had answered, thank God. Just a photo or two she had never seen. And she didn't ask to see them again. And I left them in the very same place, just in case she needed to. I told her that I had the information, and it was safe, that it was hers, and when she was ready we could look at it together if she wanted. And she said that was fine.

The holidays came. The second anniversary of him going into care. The second anniversary of the fact that they told us about all the support that would be accessed, and the second anniversary of fuck all. He went off on holiday with the foster carers. On an aeroplane. For the first time. We were asked to sign a letter of permission eventually, that said The SS had parental responsibility, to which we pointed out they didn't. We effing did. And because we did, we wanted to make sure he was sorted in case anything went wrong. "But, but, we have been using this form for years" they cried. They finally went to their legal department who said yes, the form was entirely wrong. Oops. So they used a version with appropriate amendments. They told us he didn't have an EHIC (that little card that in theory entitles you to healthcare) after they had all left to go on hollibobs. Frustrating and upsetting though all this crap was, it was all serving to prove to us that we had done the right thing. We literally could not have proper responsibility for Boy. If anything, anything, happened, it would be our legal responsibility, and the way things were going, we could not be sure that something was not going to happen. Nothing did happen of course. So that was all right then. Because nothing happened. But if it had, then what?

I had asked the Social Worker to explain a little about how Boy seemed to her when she had seen him, a couple of days after we had. I wanted to understand whether there was a problem, and why he would have acted the way he did, when things seemed to have been going well. After a prompt she emailed to say that she had seen him, and there might have been some toilet problem the morning we saw him (when they don't actually go into detail it doesn't really help, but I am wondering if this actually was code for smearing poo everywhere, which is something Boy would do when he was little, and is not unheard of in traumatised children, but I don't know). The other thing she said was that she had spoken to him, and unprompted he had said that "we were not his parents", he did not want to see us, we "asked him questions", we were "not nice", and he only wanted to see his sister. We have no idea what the Social Worker said back, we do not know what prompted this pronouncement, but it seemed that he was saying this type of thing to anyone who would listen. Except to us. When with us he wanted to play football, talked about people at school, asked to have ice-cream, told us about his latest computer game, sang songs, danced, climbed trees, demanded piggy backs, said "fuck" and mercilessly poked and criticised his sister to try to get a rise from her. We basically responded to this latest round of they are shitbags, by reminding the social worker that his sister, and therefore we, would likely be the most enduring relationship in his life, long after any Foster Care placement, and we owed it to him and his sister to encourage this relationship in a positive way, in fact it was their duty to promote "contact", and if they were not helping him to deal with his realities, and he was able to stop his new world clashing with his old one, then he would never be able to be comfortable in his own skin.

Legal Beagle Required

Second Summer without Boy passed. We had no news. Well actually no communication whatsoever about him. Apart from asking us to contribute to the thinking about his schooling (an afterthought actually as the flaming document had already been written), and being invited to a meeting in the middle of the Summer holidays to discuss our proposition to The SS that they pursue a care order, we heard not a dickie bird. We had one of those Summers of dreams, me, Hub, Girl, Dog, where the sun shone, we had family staying, saw friends, had sand under our feet, good food, and made some good memories. Girl, I and Dog went away for a whole bleeding month. Hub joined us for two weeks, and it was genuinely lovely. Dog spent days walking sideways, and didn't even roll in any cowpats. And then we returned. To more silence. Bearing in mind that Boy was starting secondary school, well a Secondary Centre for Autistic children anyway. Not momentous or anything. But then, he wasn't going to be going where he thought. Not joining his fellow classmates where he had visited, but being put into the special school. Apparently he had been told. We weren't allowed to tell him, they did it. How he reacted we did not know.

We hadn't seen him, or heard about him for two months due to the Summer break, but the contact date with him was set. We were told that the foster carers would definitely no longer be bringing him. Remember we had been told that the first time this happened it was due to illness. Well the second time no-one was really sure, but it seemed to be due to illness. Again. Anyway nothing to do with them not wanting, or being encouraged to, engage with us. But what could we say, we couldn't make a big fuss at the risk of antagonising anyone, and if that is how they wanted to play it then fine, at least Girl and Boy could see each other.

When a Thursday arrived, before the Saturday contact day, with no update I guess we should have wondered, but that night we had an email from Mr Unusual, which in itself was slightly odd. Apparently he had had a message from the foster carers social worker saying that Boy didn't want to come to see us on the Saturday. They were going to make every effort to persuade him but didn't hold out much hope. Now at this point your mind goes into overdrive. Let's think about this for a minute. What's changed so much that we find ourselves here? It was going well with Boy. OK so there were the slight complications with the carers, but he's the focus. Is it one of those unhappy coincidences that at the same time they stopped speaking to us, and started sending him to see us with someone else he started the negative commenting to others about us? Who knows. But the fact is we ended up being phoned by The SS on the Saturday morning at 8am, when we should have left to meet him, to be told that that he refused to get in the car. We were told that the foster carers had deployed their therapeutic side to try to persuade him because they knew how important contact was. It felt a little hollow. So we didn't see Boy. And that was the precedent set, right there, right then. Boy had control. And that was not actually a positive for him, or anyone else.

Why would he change his mind next time? When was the next time? What were they doing to get him help? No-one had bothered to do any life story work with him for two years, so his past and all the good and not so good people in his life morphed into a blob, that he could parcel up and move on from. He had begun the process of properly reinventing himself, again. In reality I felt that The SS should be working to arrange the contact for the next week, but nobody asked, the Anti-Social Worker had apparently properly disappeared. We didn't even know if he had a social worker. In fact nobody told us anything. So there you go. Job done.

Whilst this fiasco was allowed to happen our fateful meeting with The SS occurred with Mr Smarm and a really important Biggie Bigwig. They really were pushing out the enormous guns. I commented that the meeting took place on the third floor no less, to be told that the public were not normally allowed, but they didn't think we'd "kick off" so that was OK! Probably because the IRO had told them we were posh. A two hour meeting at which the same thing is repeated again, just to someone higher up The SS ladder, feels like your life ebbing away. We gave our thoughts, referred them back to our "lengthy" letter, and told them nothing had changed. Their actions meant that he was outside of our control and this was the threshold for a Care Order. We couldn't go on fighting every step of the way. They had not fulfilled their legal responsibilities, and we had no choice but to give up. They win. Well, sort of. In fact they couldn't get their heads round it. This was probably more unknown territory. In order to pursue the Care Order in that way, they would have to admit they were at fault, and air their laundry in public and in front of a judge and Lord knows they didn't want to do that.

The meeting ended with them asking whether we intended to make a formal complaint and if so perhaps we should deal with that first. We said that is a matter for us, and this takes precedence. So off to "Legal" they were going to trot, and get back to us. Biggie Bigwig suggested we needed an advocate… and that we would get legal aid. I pointed out that this would only be if they began care proceedings. At least I sounded like I knew my onions, and it did silence her for a second. Not that that helped at all.

Two weeks later we got a letter, with the rider that this was going on record and if we had any comments they would sit alongside it on his file. Oh dear. This new instalment in the long line of slightly wrong (is it possible to be a bit wrong…?) documents. Mr Smarm wrote that we had said this, that, and the other, which blatantly was incorrect. The upshot was that they said that Boy could not be classed as "beyond parental control" because he didn't live with us, and therefore they would be relying on the second option for a Care Order should they pursue one. That being that he was at risk of, or subject to "significant harm" when the Section 20 was enacted. And that we needed to be prepared for this in Court, and the effect it would have. Excuse me? Somewhat threatening I thought. And also I believe that if The SS suspected that a child was subject to harm they had to investigate within 48hrs of being made aware. Which they in no way had. In fact we had called the original meeting to discuss the way forward, whilst he was living with us, where they had completely no support. So I was unsure how they thought they were going to rely on this. And in fact therefore I couldn't work out how they ever thought they were going to get a Care Order. Or how they did it for other children in a Section 20 placement, if every time they had to prove it was the parents', or adoptive parents' fault. So he would be left in limbo, unless we agreed to lie. And this limbo is what judges in these cases were objecting to.

We started to wonder whether we should get legal people properly involved ourselves. We had no idea what was going to happen next. No idea when, if, we would ever see Boy. When would someone actually speak to us. And it took its toll. We had always put up with things, loudly mind, but carried on whatever, because we thought we could do the right thing. Clearly this couldn't go on. This was going to impact on Girl too.

We responded to the letter, and they had another meeting with a barista. Lovely. Oops sorry of course they meant a Barrister. Apparently they decided they could now find the basis to definitely meet the threshold for a Care Order. What had changed? Nothing as far as we knew, but apparently we should have been grateful that they were not going to pursue it because we were working with them. Basically the threat was that they would be happy to tell a judge that we were neglectful parents, but if we stopped challenging them they wouldn't do that and the situation could remain as it was. I asked if I could have access to the meeting minutes, which could be allowed, in law, if the chairperson agreed. Not possible Mr Smarm said, "I will not be releasing them to you". And by the way it is strongly recommended you supply all the information you have been asked for, so that there is no delay in providing the support Boy needs. Absolute Barstool. This was the new way. So no going in front of a judge unless we completely stopped our support and effort, and this would then prove we were incapable and give them grounds. It is emotional blackmail and deeply troubling and without integrity.

If I may indulge myself in some of my quotes at this point. If only to prove to myself that I am not quite “one wave short of a shipwreck” in the words of our dear Freddie Mercury. There was a report published for the Department for Education, in 2014 called “Beyond the Adoption Order: challenges, intervention and adoption disruption. By Julie Selwyn (University of Bristol School For Policy Studies) and others, it discussed the background to adoption difficulties and failure, and the research involved actual real people going through those experiences. And written by clever academical people. I expect it was read with disbelief. The report talked about knife hiding incidents (yes, we had that), allegations made against adoptive parents (tick), the pressure placed on adult relationships (erm, yes), how assessments were made but no services resulted (thankyou), the inability to access CAMHS (really?!), the failure of authorities to understand how genuinely desperate families were (indeed), the reluctance to provide respite for adoptive parents (what a fight), and then that looming threat of child protection investigations surrounding the lack of emotional warmth shown to children.

This was us. And it was published while we were going through it. We could have been the people quoted. We weren’t by the way. But I get angry when I think about it, because six or seven years later I see no tangible change. Which means there are probably still people like us struggling and suffering. ARSE. The issues have been recognised and identified but no lessons have been learned.

In this new climate, a new social worker did appear, as if by magic. This was going to make everything better. And we had better take note, and do what she said, said they, in almost those words. Energetic, and motivated, she was going to grip everyone. And she bloody tried. A therapist was found, but decided not to do any life story work, and focus on the here and now. The Indescribable Reviewing Officer went off sick, and the temporary replacement decided not to see us for the six monthly review meeting. Mr Unusual went off sick but that was no problem, because he was now replaced by an understudy, who we would never need to speak to anyway. Christmas came and went. We knew not what Boy had been given, we asked what he might want, something that would be special, and were not told. We got no updates on Boy. We had no idea how he genuinely was, where he had been, what he was doing. Boy who? The Boy we couldn't see. He had become a stranger. Not brilliant. But the good news was that we still retained full parental responsibility! Here we go again. The whole thing SNAFU. This was not an improvement.

It's A Different Language

So the last few months have been interesting ones. Dog started falling over, but is still appreciating being very much alive, especially because Grandma and Grandpa have been staying. Grandpa's feet being the world's best cushion and Grandma's ginger biscuits better than any Pedigree Chum might invent. Girl began her final year of primary school and it felt a bit like I know what I am doing and a bit like I'm still trying to learn Swahili but my dictionary is Mongolian. She was excited to be going back, to be at the top of the school, with all the cool swagger of a "pre-teen" and then again the just hidden wide-eyed and innocent childish side. She'll be great, I know it.

But then I got to thinking. As I did my daily trek to school and back for the umpteenth year, walked through the playground, and knew exactly where to be, and when, and said hello to peoples various. As she came sauntering out grabbing me in the rugby tackle she does every time I pick her up, I looked around at all the other people, mums and dads, and siblings, and grandparents, and other folks and thought, this doesn't feel normal. I act it, but that's what I do. I realised that my life has been dominated for so long by the dreadful situation we have been in, the one that I can't talk to most people about, that I have missed such a lot of normality.

When the children arrived and we started being parents, with all the excitement of those with new babies, we were full of hope, and expectations about the life we would have. I looked forward to engaging with other mums and being part of their gang. And I did a bit. Although I hadn't had the going through nursery experience with Boy, people were welcoming, and I got to know quite a few of them. When things started to go awry I started to keep people at arm's length, I suppose because I thought they wouldn't understand, or would judge. Because Boy didn't make friends I did try to sort of force it through being ever so nice and hoping that people would invite him over, or to a party. I tried to get him into things, and he would kick off or play up. He got the reputation and because I didn't have the friends through pregnancy, birth, nursery thing, I had nothing to fall back on. No-one knew me, and would therefore overlook things. Also because we ended up spending so much energy fighting The SS or whoever, there was no energy left for us. And when he moved out I spent some time wondering what to say, how to put it. People didn't know the situation, so trying to explain the whole thing when they were just passing the time of day was too much. So it went unsaid. At least openly. A few people knew, and they probably talked about it, I don't have a clue. But after only a few weeks no-one asked. So that was that. Since then the struggle to make sure he is OK, is still there for us. And I have limited fight left. So I haven't bothered to force myself on people I have "known" for years, but always been slightly distanced from. I haven't joined the Friends of the School. I haven't been myself. I have quietly gone about business as usual.

So now I'm not part of the mummy set as I should be, as I wanted to be, and would have been. I'm kind of waiting for secondary school to start where there's no history. Where I don't have to be fabulous. Oh I have changed. And probably not for the better. I now watch what I say. I do the bland response thing a lot, because I learned that tone of voice is important to children who dysregulate. I am not the same excitable nut that I was I suppose. I am more serious. Because I am pretending not to care about all that crap. I don't need anyone else. I do things my way and everything is fine. Nothing to see. I won't rely on any other people, outside of our family unit.

They let you down. I spoke to Hub about this earlier, and he sort of did a nod / sigh and said yes, things were soured. I feel for him too. He would have been a great dad to Boy, the greatest. Girl thinks he is, and so do I, but he hasn't been able to do all the things he hoped either. The memories which should be good, are often as he said, soured. What a place to be in.

I still wonder to myself sometimes whether it was us, whether we were just not capable. Girl will have none of that. She has no doubts about whose daughter she is. She never entertains the idea that she would be anywhere else. Even if her brother is talked about. He isn't here, she is. As far as she is concerned she belongs. Apart from our parents, and close friends, she is the only one who actually seems to understand why things happened, and why she feels in a better place now than before. It really is quite incredible, she will openly talk about being adopted, and why, but there is never an inkling of any other life being possible. Just occasionally she reminds me of Boy. They have very similar facial expressions and characteristics. And when she is in one, she will pull a face, or say something which jolts my memory. And these moments are the reminders of the past. And the moments where something in me wonders, should I worry, is history going to repeat itself? Is nature too strong? And then I think well, you know how to deal with this, and we learn and are more conscious now than ever that life isn't a picnic. And nobody else you know has your experience, so get over yourself. Just be grateful for what you have and get a backbone. OK so she is still in therapy … not your fault. She still cannot regulate herself sometimes … not your fault. She may have issues later in life ... not your fault. She is polite … OK, do blame me. She is quirky … I'll take that one. She is happy … bring it on. She laughs at my jokes, she and I know I am actually hilarious and should be on the stage.

Regarding being useless parents, I have grumbled all along about people saying how wonderful you are when really you are wishing they would put a sock in it, because in reality they don't know what goes on, and are still thinking of the fairy tale part of the story where you rescued two children. And you want to tell them but you can't because that would be unfair and cruel. Everyone needs a fairy tale. However the people who I do take it from are the foster carers who we received the children from. Remember them? I am still in contact with them. We don't talk about the issues, rather preferring just to exchange greetings and news. They don't criticise, they don't judge, they still want to be in touch. It means a lot to me. At first I apologised for failing, but they were not having any of that. I send them school photos so they can see the progress. That's important because they were important.

In one of those moments of waiting, which you seem to do a lot of with children (and husbands), I was flicking through a photo album. I'm saying that because I wish it was an album, I actually mean my phone photos, which apparently it's not cool to print out. Anyway I looked back over the period we have had children, seven years of memories, and I have to say it would make an interesting montage at my funeral. Fascinating, as Mr Spock would say. It makes me both happy and wistful... wisty? There's good, bad and even ugly. All important memories though. It's like a Christmas wish list for a crazy Santa. Subjects include: crabs, Dog, a bouncy donkey, Dog, a hookah pipe, a metre of chewed bed, a number of folk festivals, ukuleles in abundance, a giant Yorkshire pudding, a rainbow, half a toothbrush (other half eaten), pig's trotters, Dog, barefoot mud walk, the moon, a Banksy, four pairs of destroyed shoes, cheese, Professor Brian Cox, a smashed Ipad, Dog, a witch's head, Elvis, a medieval toilet, ice-creams various, a goat, eyeball cakepops, some chewed buttons, candy floss, a small hand reared bird, jam, Nutella, lots of Dog. That tells me that life went on. That's a snippet. Partly because I can't find my phone at the right time to capture the moment, partly because there are so many I cherry picked. I am happy with all that stuff, things that were eaten tell a story, and are still memories.

In all the discussions, meetings, legal talk, everyone has representation. It becomes clear that there are sides. We have always tried to be open and honest and work for Boy, to get everyone championing him. But you end up in a kind of arena, where there is opposition. You realise that in one corner is The SS and their might. All the important people form a big galactic force and how do you deal with that? If you disagree or challenge, you are side-lined, seen as troublemakers. Because you see, they have to blame someone, and you are easy. Nobody cares how sad you are, how guilty you feel. So sometimes this results in you joining forces and feeling empowered and united together, and other times it makes you argumentative because you are so riled that everyone gets a piece of it, and because you are really just two humans with different opinions which are equally as important. I think that if you can stick together through it then you must be very resilient. What doesn't kill you makes you stronger eh?

Together you portray an unemotional side in discussions or when you are telling the story. Maybe we should have rolled around the floor having a breakdown, but that's not what we do. Behind that hard wall, and to each other you are genuine and hurting. A new friend hearing the story for the first time, and wiping her eyes, said how distressing it all was, and that she felt like hugging us. "Yes it is" we agreed, but "no hugging required" we said. It reminded us how steely we have become, out of necessity, with the dark humour that is so loved, and also so loathed. You tell a story about how you looked up and proclaimed "have I not been tested enough?!" And then the wheel literally fell off your car and ambled past you down the road (true story!). The tears are dried and everybody is OK again. Much merriment about "that's life", "riding high in April, shot down in May" (Frank Sinatra I believe). Upset averted. Just saying.

I have a thing for Brian Cox. I never met him, Hub did, hence the photo I have of the lovely couple. Was I jealous? The closest I came was at a D-Ream concert in 1997. "Things can only get better" they said. I believed it. But by God things can get worse before they do Brian. In a more scientific guise he said that "there are too many people in this world who want to be right. And too few who just want to know." (Brian Cox. Force of Nature, 1997). I love him even more. Sometimes I want to prove me right about Boy, but I know that it should be more important just to know, to understand. I don't think anyone really does, and there has been too much trying to prove blame, fault … I am definitely guilty of that. And it doesn't help. And won't help. So we have now tried to stop fighting it.

Don't get me wrong, we are now a great threesome. Me, Hub, Girl. Oh, sorry Dog, I know you are still there. We are a great three and a half some. We do stuff. We laugh (bark) and we know each others foibles (smells). If you really think about it, something probably happens every day to make you smile, at least inwardly. Today I discovered that Hub had found one of his shoes on the roof of his car, having driven around for at least two weeks wondering where they were. Someone probably got a bit of a shock when a blue suede shoe bounced off their bonnet at 70 miles an hour on the M1 motorway. We have a good life. But there is something that will always be missing, and the spectre of it looms still, all of a sudden reminding you of your failures, or if not your failures, the failures of the system, or if not that, raises the worries in you about the realistic future of the child you promised to look after forever, and now struggle to even even see. You know that there is no going back. You know that all the decisions were made for the right reasons. You know that you couldn't have fought harder. You know what it did to you. But that doesn't make it feel better. And why should it. The only thing you can tell yourself is that Girl is a blossom. You look at her, or people say I know where she gets that from, and you think, they mean me. And she thinks it too. And that is good. And that I know.

I wondered what would end this story, what would make me write my final full stop. Would it be at the point when they got a Care Order for Boy? Will I just wake up one day and think, "that's it, all sorted, we can now relax"? Is there going to be some event that signifies an ending? I think no, no and no. I'll just have to stop talking to you. I can't bring myself to take you with us on the next bit of this farce. The Court proceedings which I thought would be inevitable. Probably the mud-slinging, us getting upset, them being offensive to be defensive. What's the point of that? It's the end. As it is, bruised and battered we have spent seven years of our life trying to do the right thing for a child who we had longed for and fallen in love with. We failed. The right thing has not been done. The supposed therapeutic help he was supposed to get, that the Section 20 would bring after we failed to get it when he was with us, never materialised, he has not been helped to understand himself, he has no idea who he was or is, he has not been diagnosed with anything, yet is in a special school because mainstream won't accommodate him. The EHCP that his first school fought so hard for has unbelievably not been updated for 4 years, needless to say we have asked! If I may be bold he lives with people who do not need to be interested in his past. Hub and I are still here. Girl does well. Dog? Yes. Makes her presence felt still. If you are plant pot-shaped and no higher than a foot from the ground, then you still need to be very careful.

I'd like to end on a high, but I fear I'm going to end on a why. Why does this keep happening? With such a body of evidence out there about the difficulties faced with adopting older children, sibling groups, traumatised youngsters, why when the call for help is made, is the response so woeful? The financially overstretched climate might explain it, but it doesn't make it right. And in truth if they had worked out the cost of helping us and Boy, or looked at the charitable grants that were available, and taken that leap and supported us, then we probably could have coped. They would be probably £60k a year (and rising) better off, Boy would (in our opinion) be in a more positive place, and the therapeutic foster carers could have been used for another child in desperate need. But this would have taken vision, and looking at whole life cost, not the penny pinching annual budgets that have to be split so many ways, leading to a resource-led, not needs-led (put the child at the centre) kind of service.

There is such a lack of empathy, a need to blame, a lack of support. There have been glimmers of hope, and I am sure that there are many families who have received timely support preventing disasters like ours. So we are a statistic. An unpublished one (so one that doesn't actually exist) but nevertheless one for whom it went wrong. We need to pick up the pieces of our jigsaw and carry on. Albeit one of those jigsaws with one frigging bit missing. Story of my life.

Childish Words of Wisdom

My friend said the other day that it's been a tough and busy year, and they thought they would jet off to the Caribbean after Christmas… not being funny but try having the time we've had and then I will sympathise, I'm not wallowing in self-pity and I expect that we'll look back and be amazed at ourselves… what doesn't kill you makes you stronger doesn't it? What I wanted to ask was "in the last year have you been accused, hit, screamed at, ignored, blamed, wanted to drive off a cliff on a regular basis, been told how to live your life, had your life scrutinised, and been expected to still do the right thing, and then with all this going on made the hardest decision of your life, and then been punished for that consistently?" But I didn't say that, I just smiled and said how much they deserved a break. And then we ate cake, with no pink custard.

There are still remnants, still reminders of the momentary part of our life that really included little Boy. I found a tiny little football shirt in my drawer the other day. One day I will give it to him, it might make him genuinely smile, a bit. His school photo is still on the window ledge. It's a bit faded, but it is still there. His bike is still in the shed. He can't ride a bike nowadays. There's a box full of old school stuff, birthday cards and certificates in the loft, but nobody wants it. So I guess it will stay there until it's needed. Bit like the memories in your head, kind of put to one side, but still there to surprise you every now and then.

I can't say for sure, or maybe I can, adopting children can never feel the same as seeing those two blue lines, having them inside you for nine months, doing up your nursery, the baby shower, the birth, the bonding. It is so different, there is no identifiable bond, no family traits to be passed on. But has its own excitements, beautiful moments, and celebratory occasions, but any child you adopt is never going to be "all" yours. They have baggage, some of it you didn't know they'd unwittingly smuggled into your house. Though I am to this day not sure The SS didn't know of the excess baggage, just maybe forgot to mention it. They declare it more openly now we are told! The baggage is always unpacked in some way. You may help them carry it, you may unpack it with them, they may not want to show you. Their baggage may have labels like those old suitcases, been here, there and everywhere, and it made me me.

Their baggage might have been unpacked at customs, gone through, quarantined, examined. You may or may not understand it. You may not even know. You can get along though, you can bimble through life doing your best to understand each others emotions, to be empathetic, or curious, loving and never judging. Sometimes it's not enough.

Don't talk to me about "tummy mummy". That phrase makes me cringe. It is so kind and cuddly. I'm not a tummy mummy, but I am a mummy. I said I would grow into it and I have tried to. With my daughter I am that one. I am her mummy and Hub is her daddy, that is a fact, that is without question. She knows her history, we are non-judgemental about it, she makes her own mind up, has her own opinions, lots of them. One day she might look back and have empathy, sympathy, some other pathy for her birth mother (also awful name, but what do you want me to do, that's what they call them?). That is fine (at the moment). We know what it is like (vicariously through family) when someone finds their birth family and idealises them, and gravitates towards them. That has to be OK. We are all human, and in reality we can never understand another's feelings, we can try, but to not really know our heritage must be so difficult. And then there is that greener grass. But for now all we can do is try and be family, and enjoy it, and be frustrated by it in equal measures. And see where it gets us. My daughter is mine, my son is not mine any more, maybe he never was. I do not know him, he does not know me. I can only advocate for him and hope that he can be the best he can be, and know that he was too broken for me to help, without my own help. I am human. Do we deserve the treatment we got? Did we do it wrong? Are we all the things they said we were? Did we burst our own karma bubble because of our own behaviour? Were we horrid? I hope not. Our daughter doesn't think so, and that's good enough for me. I know how she feels. I will quote, "I wouldn't worry mummy, one day you'll come in handy". Yes, yes I will darling, thank you for that.

The thing is that lots of lives have been spoiled. We got what we wanted, and it went so horribly wrong. The beautiful beginnings, with lashings of lemonade and pink custard, the growing up of our glorious daughter, watching her learn and develop. All the memories of that are tainted with the horror that we almost cannot think about. We can't compartmentalise her part, they were both there. So many occasions were affected. Now, call it PTSD, call it whatever you want, I would never say that to most people for fear of being over-dramatic, but we verge on the hyper-vigilant ourselves. Sometimes Girl does things and we look for the cause, where we should just think, well she is only ten. I think I know what a normal family is like. I think I come from one. I don't have one. I act normal (don't argue, I do). But often inside my head I feel like I am acting. Fake it until you make it, Young Psycholady used to say. I don't know if I will ever make it. I love my daughter. She loves me back, and her Daddy. When people compliment her on her wavy hair, she will say "I have this because of mummy". It chips another bit off your broken heart. Part of me is ice now. We dance, we sing, we roll on the floor, we eat weird stuff, we tell rude jokes about bottoms. But I have that hard part of me, that is frozen. Because if I let it defrost I will get hurt, and I don't want any more pain. I just want to be mum. Like my mum, or mum's mum. That is what I will never be, maybe to Girl I am. But not to myself. She is my pride, and mostly my joy. I don't know where we will go, how things will turn out, for us, or for her. I hope she will be OK. Hey I didn't do the things that were done in the first years of her life, or his. I wasn't there. So I won't blame me for those things.

It's my birthday today. I am 45. Five years ago I sent my babysitter, husband and daughter out to get her away from the screaming boy that was raging in the house. My 40th birthday dinner did not take place, it couldn't. This time I am sitting here peacefully talking to you, Dog's here walking sideways making smells, daughter around somewhere playing, husband on his way. He is cooking a nice meal tonight. We're staying in, because we want to, because we are happy to be at home, because it's not a scary place any more.

I just read a book about empowerment of women, with a contribution from a friend of mine. I was thinking secretly to myself, you need to think like that. I have a good job, I've jumped out of an aircraft, learned to play an instrument, ride a motorbike and ski, not at the same time, took my mother across the world on her trip of a lifetime, deployed to a war zone, trekked to Everest, learned to speak French, still got the grande dame of a house (note to self … she needs her makeup retouching in places), and still have the pleasure of an ancient, set in her ways, slightly unsteady on her feet, and momentously stinky, deaf to most normal noises, with some impressive cataracts, rather wonderful and contented old dog. My therapist tells me I have PTSD, and secondary trauma. Can you tell? You wouldn't if you met me.

So this is my book. There was a beginning, and a middle, but it doesn't have an end. If you have stuck with me as I told the story, you will know what you think. This is my truth, not anyone else's, although my Dad told me to get it out there, Mother told me to do the same to somehow end it … and Hub went over it and told me what to take out, he let me leave a lot in, brave man! But I've said it now, and it's out there. No going back. If seven years ago you had been told how to be a mum, then become a mum, and been advised how to mum specifically, then told how you were pretty much failing as a mum, then literally failing to be a mum, and being informed that you were not thought of as a mum, and then criticised for the way you mummed. For seven years I have listened to other people telling me what I should and shouldn't be doing. The proof of the pudding? Complicated. One rose, one sunk. In the same oven. Please don't try to analyse it. It is what it is. And we have to believe that we made the right choices, and that the last seven years mean something or will do one day. There's a little girl who is blossoming, that gives us strength. We are laughing again, that is important. We walk around with all this stuff going round in our heads, but we are actually OK. If Boy chooses to make contact with us, there's a part of our heart that will always be reserved for him.

An after-thought

Dear Resilient Reader

If you have persevered through the sorry tale I have just told, then thank you, I do appreciate it. Thank you also to Hub for reading it 42 times, and for toning me down. And my lovely friend Y for reading it too, I didn't mean to cause tears. I realised in the middle of writing this, that I all I wanted to do was to get our story out there, whatever it looked like. And at times that could be quite hurtful, which was never my intention. I know that people will form their own opinion about what the "right" thing to do might have been. Some people will empathise, some will criticise. I'm not going to argue. It's up to them. We are all human and as you can't get someone to live your life for you, all you can do is be honest.

Not enough is said about this side of adoption, except it seems between the people it is happening to. We hope that you never have to walk in our shoes. But the more people that know, the more it will be talked about ...

maybe. Perhaps someone listening will actually hear. Questions might be answered and maybe when things get tricky, go wrong, reveal themselves, maybe, just maybe, someone might get a better bloody response than we did. And maybe, more timely support might be forthcoming. I still don't know what our solution would have been. Everyone's will be different. But no-one should judge, except the judges. There are so many sodding maybes, unknowns, and perhaps. But that's life I suppose. You just never know, so you have to go for it, you have to try. Good people will right now be launching into their new lives, full of hope, as we did.

But just remember if all else fails you can stick a plant pot on your head and run around the garden for a bit. I think I'll go and do that now.

Thanks and all the best

H

Printed in Great Britain
by Amazon

61616420R10160